THE PARABLES
OF JOSHUA

THE PARABLES

OF JOSHUA

JOSEPH F. GIRZONE

DOUBLEDAY

New York   London   Toronto   Sydney   Auckland

PUBLISHED BY DOUBLEDAY
a division of Random House, Inc.
1540 Broadway, New York, New York 10036

DOUBLEDAY and the portrayal of an anchor with a dolphin are
trademarks of Doubleday, a division of Random House, Inc.

Library of Congress Cataloging-in-Publication Data
Girzone, Joseph F.
The parables of Joshua/Joseph F. Girzone.—1st ed.
p. cm.
1. Joshua (Fictitious character)—Fiction. I. Title.
PS3557.I77 P37 2001
813'.54—dc21
00-063919

ISBN 0-385-49511-0
Printed in the United States of America
April 2001
First Edition
1 3 5 7 9 10 8 6 4 2

PREFACE

THERE IS much said and many things written about
Gospel parables. They are nice to read because their
stories are far removed from modern life, and rarely have
the stunning effect that they must have had when Jesus
first told them, particularly when you consider the audiences. I have heard the most callous people comment with
such great piety on the parables. I could not help but wonder if we haven't made parables pleasant-sounding fables
about human situations long past, but with no present-day
meaning. We don't see investors today scratching around
a neighbor's property for some long-forgotten treasure,
hoping they can make a killing if they buy the field. They
may involve themselves in shady stock deals, and inside in-
formation, but digging around a neighbor's property

when he is not at home is no longer a common practice. Our treasures are now kept in banks where the accounts are insured. We might occasionally see someone wandering along a beach with a metal detector hoping to find a few coins or perhaps a watch, but that's just play. Or who in our day ever heard of a farmer going out in the middle of the night to poison his neighbor's crop, a common way to eliminate competition in the old days? Crops are insured today or, if not, then usually protected by the government. The messages behind the parables are the substance of these quaint, poignant stories Jesus told with such ease. A way to make these vital messages meaningful today is to dress them in modern clothes and retell them in a way that can touch a modern audience.

In the many visits Joshua has made to so many places, he has rarely spoken the way he did during his original visit, centuries ago. He has seemed to be content just to reassure people of his Father's love, and deepen their awareness of the reality of the supernatural. However, when approached and questioned, Joshua has always responded in a frank and forthright manner, telling stories in the form of parables, as he did many centuries before. As times and circumstances have changed since his original appearance on earth, his stories have also changed as he has tried to clarify issues frequently debated among his followers. Let me tell you some of these parables.

THE PARABLES
OF JOSHUA

THE PARABLE
OF THE WEALTHY ARTIST

ON ONE OCCASION, as Joshua was talking to a crowd that had gathered around him, a woman spoke up and bluntly asked him what he thought of the Church. Calm and unruffled, Joshua replied, "The kingdom of God is like a man who had great wealth and power. He controlled vast territories and whole populations throughout the world. His wealth was beyond measure and, indeed, seemed without limit. He was, however, not concerned with power, or even with his wealth. His joy was in creating living masterpieces of art and sculpture. But in spite of his great possessions, he was alone, and had no one with whom to share his joy. Disguising himself as an ordinary person, he sought out those with whom he could share his life. Dressed in plain clothes and living in a simple manner, he began his search. He approached those who appeared intelligent and wise in the things of the world. "Certainly these men and women will be friends with whom I can share my life," he said to himself, and he approached them.

"What does he want of us?" they asked themselves. They were suspicious and looked down on him as a person of no value or use to themselves, so they shunned him. Others he met were highly intelligent persons of science and possessed knowledge of many things. However, he soon found that they were enchanted with their own intelligence and saw no reason to allow this simple man into their lives. He would be a nuisance and could contribute nothing to their circle of learned colleagues. They too shunned him. Others were persons of great importance and had many friends in high places. He approached them, thinking they would, without doubt, appreciate his friendship, but they were ashamed even to be seen with him. They too shunned him.

"Discouraged by the shallow vision of all these intelligent people, the rich man decided to look among ordinary people. They were kind and friendly toward him and welcomed him into their friendship. Taking him into their homes, they shared with him their meager possessions and their simple food, and allowed him into their lives, without any question or concern about his status. However, even among these good people, some soon tired of him, and found excuses to avoid him. But to those who opened their hearts and allowed him to share in their friendship, he revealed his true identity and shared with them his life

and the awesome world in which he lived. When the others saw what had happened, they were beside themselves
with grief that with all their smug intelligence they had
failed to perceive the greatness hidden beneath the
stranger's simple manner. What they had searched for all
their lives was nothing compared with the riches and the
glory and power the rich man shared so freely with all
those simple people. And that is the way it will be with
those who, when the Savior comes knocking, see in him
nothing of value, and so turn him away, and continue to
walk in darkness."

The Parable
of the Pilgrims' Guide

O N ANOTHER DAY as Joshua was standing on the shore of a great lake, he remarked to the small crowd that was with him, "The kingdom of heaven is like adventurers who wanted to cross a great sea. On the shore was a guide charged by his captain with the responsibility of directing pilgrims to their destination. He knew well the destination and the safest way to arrive there. After giving pilgrims careful instructions he warned them that the voyage was long and dangerous, and without proper guidance, they could become lost along the way. But they should not be afraid because the gentle breeze along the course would take them safely through dangerous waters and carry them to their destination. One man said to himself, 'I am strong and wise. I know the waters better than he. I can find my own way. Why should I trust a breeze to guide me? And, besides, I do not like the guide. I will follow my own directions.' So he, and others like him, took off in a boat of their own design. But after many days of toiling against adverse winds, and with no one to guide them, they became confused and exhausted, and gave up. There were others who followed after them. Most of them met with the same fate.

"Another group listened to the guide. They considered his words but were reluctant to follow his advice. 'We are afraid of the water. We cannot swim and, besides, it is too far for us to row. Why should we follow the guide's directions? We will walk around the sea.' So, they began walking. After many months, they became weary and exhausted and could no longer endure the hardship. Realizing it was impossible for them to reach their destination on their own strength, they too gave up.

"There were still others on the shore who listened to the guide and took his advice. They knew they could not row across such an impossible expanse of water without guidance and without support. They also realized that they could not survive the impossible walk around the sea. They decided to follow the guide's directions. Moored on the shore was a large sailboat, which the guide used on his own trips. He told the group they were welcome to use it. They were delighted.

"As they were about to leave, they asked others if they would like to come with them, as there was still room.

" 'No,' they replied, 'we will go on our own. We are

all going to the same place. It makes no difference how we get there. We will meet you on the other side.'

"So, freeing the boat from its moorings, the group set sail and carefully followed the guide's directions, always letting themselves be guided by the gentle breeze in difficult times. Though the voyage was not easy, they never lost heart as they were gently guided through calm and difficult times.

"Finally they arrived at their destination. The most breathtaking vision unfolded before their eyes. It was a kingdom of magnificent splendor. As they emerged from the boat, they were greeted by the inhabitants, who were thrilled to see them. Immediately, a celebration was arranged at which they were formally welcomed. After many days, they looked for the others who left when they did, but they had not yet arrived."

"Would you explain the parable to us?" Joshua's friend Pat asked him.

"Yes," Joshua told him. "The great sea is the span of a person's life on earth. The destination is the kingdom of heaven after death. The captain is the Savior. The guide is the apostles Jesus left to teach his people. Those who rejected their guidance and decided to walk to their destination are those who knowingly reject the teachers Jesus sent and choose instead to follow their own lights. They soon become weary and confused and eventually lose their way. Those who disliked the guide and his instructions and followed a manual of their own are those who have rejected the guides whom the Savior has given them and, building boats of their own, follow guides of their own making. The sailboat is the Church, ever guided by the gentle breeze of the Holy Spirit, and in its understanding of God's Word, which will always be available to carry people safely to the kingdom of heaven across."

PARABLES
OF THE KINGDOM

O R AGAIN, the path to the kingdom of heaven is like a majestic oceanliner carrying passengers to a faraway land. Many of the officers on the ship were good people. A few, however, were dishonorable. There were also on the ship righteous passengers who were offended by the behavior of the dishonorable crewmen and decided they would no longer travel with them. One night, when all were asleep, they unhitched the lifeboats and quietly slipped them into the ocean. Abandoning the ship, they attempted to make the long and treacherous voyage on their own. After drifting aimlessly for many days without provisions, some were fortunate to be rescued.

Or again, the kingdom of heaven is like a group of people lost in a jungle. For days and weeks they fought their way through heavy brush and impossible conditions, always fearful of poisonous snakes and wild animals. On the verge of despair, they one day encountered a wise man. They knew neither where he came from nor where he was going. Approaching him, they inquired if he could point for them the way to safety. The wise man thought and thought for the longest time, continually looking over the desperate group. He thought of telling the whole group the way out, but decided against it, realizing that if he told them all, each would understand his message in a different way, and they would end up arguing and fighting and perhaps killing one another. So the wise man decided to pick one person who was wise and concerned for the group, and shared with him alone the directions out of the jungle. Then, the wise man left to continue on his way in the opposite direction. For a while the group was happy to follow the leader whom the wise man had appointed, but as time passed, some became disgruntled and decided that they would rather find their own way through the jungle. So, they parted ways. Farther along the path, a few more decided they would follow their own lights. They also left and went their own way. Those who remained loyal to the leader ultimately found their way to safety, while the others wandered aimlessly through the jungle.

THE PARABLE
OF THE UNWORTHY
SHEPHERD

ONE SUNDAY MORNING, in a small mountain village, Joshua and his friends were talking in front of church after services. Clergy were standing nearby listening to the conversation. Pat told Joshua of a friend who was deeply hurt because her pastor had told her she was not a good woman, that she was a sinner.

Joshua then told them a parable. "A woman had three little children. The man with whom she lived cared nothing for her and rarely came home. The woman asked her pastor to baptize her baby. He refused, saying she was not a good woman because she did not obey all the laws of the Church. Whenever she went to church, she begged the pastor to baptize her baby. He always refused, insisting that she first marry the man with whom she was living. This she could not do because she strongly believed the man no longer loved her, but she was afraid to leave him out of concern for the children. The woman appealed to the pastor's superiors. They refused to consider her request. The woman was devastated. A short time later, the pastor died. The chief mourner was a woman to whom the pastor had been secretly married for many years, even though he had another wife and several children. A short time later the mother also died. To which one, do you think, would God show more compassion?"

One of the ministers hearing the parable blushed with shame and anger, because he knew the parable was directed at him, but could say nothing without betraying himself.

The Parable
of the Terrorist
and the Unwed Mother

ONE DAY, in a country where civil strife had been raging for centuries, a group of clergy approached Joshua, in an attempt to trap him. "Sir, we know you speak your mind whether people agree with you or not, and we admire your honesty. Should clergy approve of patriots who struggle to free their country?" Joshua, seeing their hypocrisy, proposed the following story for their consideration.

"There lived in a town a terrorist who murdered and raped innocent people under the guise of fighting to free his country. Every month the man went to church and received Communion. The priest said nothing. There were terrorists in other churches who did the same. Their priests said nothing. Nor did the bishop. In the same town, there lived a woman who had been divorced and remarried without the Church's blessing. Her husband was not of her faith and refused to submit to a church he did not believe in. The woman, however, was a good woman and had a deep love for her religion and brought up her children to be faithful to God and their religion. When she went to church, however, the priest refused to give her Communion. She was, he told her, not a good woman and was living in sin. There were many in the church who were not troubled by the priest giving Communion to the terrorist, and who praised him for his loyalty to the Church's laws in refusing the woman Communion. There were others, however, who were horrified at the priest's callousness, and thought him a hypocrite, more dedicated to Church law than to God's law of love and mercy. Eventually, they all died and went before God. I ask you, from your own knowledge of Jesus' actions in the Gospels, what do you think would be God's judgment on each of them?"

"It is very difficult to say how God would judge," they replied.

"That is because you judge by evil bias and not by God's standards," Joshua answered.

"But is not patriotism a virtue in God's eyes?" they persisted.

"When it is an expression of love of neighbor, it is

patriotism, yes. When it inspires hatred of one's neighbor and murder of innocent people, it is an evil despicable in God's eyes. Your own blindness condemns you." Joshua's interrogators walked away, furious at his answer.

THE PARABLE
OF THE TWO RICH MEN

ONE DAY, a very wealthy man who went to church every day and was highly respected in his community approached Joshua and asked him, "Does a rich man have to give away hard-earned money to the poor, who never did a decent day's work?"

Joshua responded by telling a parable. "In a great city there lived people from many nations. Among them were some who for various reasons were very poor. In the same city there lived two rich men. One man was totally dedicated to his business ventures. There was little room in his heart for God or for his family. For the poor whom he passed on the streets each day he had only contempt. His passion was to build skyscrapers and gambling casinos and plush hotels. Businessmen and -women admired his shrewdness. There was another rich man who lived in the same city. When he passed the poor on the streets each day, his heart was moved to compassion. He had in his young life accumulated vast wealth, but his wealth meant nothing to him if he could not use it to help others. So, he decided to buy up huge tracts of land. He then hired the poor people to work for him. It was his plan to demolish and rebuild that part of the city where the poor lived so they could live and work in dignity. They worked untiringly, day and night, tearing down and rebuilding their neighborhood. The rich man's architects designed schools and a clinic, a cultural center, and parks, and restored a famous old golf course to its former beauty, and built another besides, along with tennis courts and swimming pools, and places for the children to play. All these facilities were for the use of those living there and for the children as long as they did well in school. He also built stores and set up businesses for the people to operate once they were fully trained. And as in luxury developments, security guards staffed the gatehouse and patrolled the area.

"The other rich man laughed at him and said his dream was a waste of money. 'What can the poor do for you?' he sneered. To which the kind man replied, 'I expect nothing from the poor, except their willingness to work with us. However, I am concerned that one day God will ask me, not how much money I made, or what I did for my own glory, but what did I do for others.' Soon, the dream became reality, and the people who lived there were a people filled with pride. The kind man knew that God was pleased and that it was all worthwhile."

The rich man told Joshua, "That is a nice story, Joshua, but you know as well as I that it is just a pipe dream." To which Joshua responded, "It is not a tale. It is a real place that I recently visited, the accomplishment of a man with God in his heart."

THE PARABLE
OF THE BEAUTIFUL GARDEN

ONE DAY as Joshua was walking with friends along the side of a lake, they came upon a stream flowing into the lake. At the mouth of the stream were dead fish of all kinds. The odor was sickening. Joshua looked at the stream and realized it had once been pure and crystal clear, and life giving. Now it was dirty and poisoned. He looked around and saw dying trees and fallen trunks of once healthy pines and firs. Joshua's friends could see his mood changing as he scanned the site. There was a look of deep sadness at what he saw.

He spoke gently as if reminiscing, "There was once a great and generous king who designed a vast enchanted garden for his subjects. This garden extended for many miles in all directions. In the garden the king planted trees and shrubs and plants of every kind. Some were for food and some were just for beauty to give joy and pleasure to his subjects. At first the subjects admired the beautiful garden, and used the plants for food and the pure waters to quench their thirst. As time passed, there were some who realized that the plants and trees were valuable. They began to treat the garden as if it were their own. They sold many of the precious plants. They cut down the ancient trees for timber; the rare plants growing for centuries in their shade were forever destroyed, with nothing to replace them. They left in their wake poisons of all kinds, and what was once a beautiful gift of the king to his subjects was slowly becoming a dump poisonous to all forms of life, even the life of the king's subjects."

Joshua was silent for the longest time. His friends could see that he was deeply troubled by what he had just experienced. Finally, looking at them, he said, "Teach your children that everything in nature is a precious gift from a loving God. Explain to them how valuable are all the treasures in creation. They are the common heritage of all God's children and not private possessions to be exploited by a few. Those who use them should use them for the good of all."

THE PARABLE
OF THE PRECIOUS SEED

JOSHUA WAS TALKING to a crowd that had gathered around him. A woman abruptly asked him a question, which surprised the crowd. "Is it right to destroy a child's life before it is born?"

Joshua thought for a moment, then answered, "I will tell you a story. A team of scientists on an archaeological expedition found deep in the earth, frozen for millions of years, a few tiny seeds. Realizing that they were priceless living fossils, they rushed them back to the laboratory and placed them in a carefully controlled environment. After spending months analyzing other fossil specimens to see if they could identify and keep alive their precious discovery, they finally determined which type of plant it was and the climate in which it would have originally grown, and in which it might still grow. The scientists then set about preparing the necessary environment and temperature and other conditions necessary for the germination and growth of this rare and priceless plant.

"When a human life is conceived, it is a unique creation, more priceless than any fossil plant, no matter how rare. The enormous numbers of its species make it no less rare or priceless. It is a one-of-a-kind creation of God that will live not just for a limited span of time, but for eternity. Should that human life be treated with any less care and awesome devotion than were those few fossil seeds? For those without faith, it is easy to treat God's most precious gifts as trash, though for some it is just a tragic mistake."

THE PARABLE
OF THE UNFORGIVING
COMMUNITY

JOSHUA WAS HAVING breakfast one morning at a diner. Two friends from the village were sitting across from him. When they noticed him, they invited themselves over and sat down. "Good morning, Joshua!" said Charles, a good-natured, heavyset man in his late forties.

"Good morning, men!" Joshua returned with a smile.

"Hope you don't mind us sitting here with you," the man continued.

"Not at all. I enjoy company."

Usually when people approached Joshua it was not for small talk, as it was well known that Joshua rarely indulged in small talk. The men soon came around to why they wanted to talk with him.

"Joshua," Charles said, "Tom and I were just discussing a problem in my family."

"No, Joshua," Tom interrupted, "it's not a problem in the family. Charles is the problem. He's hardly talked to his sister in twenty years. Tell him the whole story, Charles."

"Well, I guess it *has* been a long time since we've really talked. Tom says I'm mean and unforgiving. I've forgiven her but I will never talk to her again. She calls and I'm civil."

"You're not even civil, Charles. You let her know you're just being charitable and that's mean. She has to come crawling to talk to you, and you make her squirm. You call that civil. That's sick, Charles."

"Let me tell you a story," Joshua said. "There was a community in a faraway land. They were kind and gentle people, each and every one. But, as in so many communities, there are happy times and painful times, so in this community there were happy times and painful times. And as in all families there are also rivalries and tense situations, so in this community there were rivalries and tensions, but they could not see in themselves the meanness they were inflicting on one another. It was always another's fault. On one occasion, a man's donkey trampled his neighbor's garden. The neighbor was furious and no matter how hard the man apologized and tried to make amends, the neighbor remained stubborn and unforgiving. Nobody in their families was allowed to talk to the others. Similar situations occurred in other families, with the same reactions. Innocent things were said or done, and no matter how much the person tried to explain, it was useless. Other community members who were on close terms with the offender were also suspect and immediately eliminated from friendly contact.

"Before long the whole village was at odds. Even close family members no longer associated or talked to one another. They would confess that it was always for the noblest reasons that they did not speak, for they were really good Christians. And as there was no possibility of any real forgiveness in the community, healing of wounds was forever impossible. The sad part of it all was that their consciences never troubled them because each day they would say a prayer for the others. And as long as they said a prayer they felt absolved from guilt. Family members died, and the others found out from strangers, often too late to express their deepest sympathy to the family. Lifetimes passed and the people of the village could no longer remember why they were not talking. They just knew they were not supposed to be friends, yet they still deeply loved and said prayers for one another. The children grew up and did not know their closest relatives, and would pass them in the streets and avoid them. They felt there was something unhealthy about them and that they should have nothing to do with them.

"One day, at Easter, at the celebration of the resurrection of the Savior, the priest looked across the congregation and saw his little parish family celebrating, but each one with a heart full of hatred and meanness. At the end of Mass, he walked down the aisle and, and instead of going outside, took a key from under his robes and locked the door of the church, then walked back to the sanctuary and faced the people.

" 'We just worshiped the Lord and professed our undying love for him. We beat our breasts in sorrow for sin, asking God's forgiveness. Well, I will tell you that what I see here before me is not a loving, caring Christian family, with hearts full of love and forgiveness, but a rabble of unrelated people with hearts full of meanness, vindictiveness, and petty hatred, carefully sugarcoated with a thousand sick excuses. How can you in conscience call yourself Christians when you have never forgiven the slightest hurts committed against you, even when unintended? Well, I have made up my mind. No one is leaving this church until you all make peace with one another. I don't care if we have to stay here until we starve. You can attack me and kill me, if you like, but I will hold this key tight in my dying hands. I will not unlock the doors of this church until we all leave here with peace and forgiveness and love in our hearts.'

"A frightful silence filled the little church. Then, after what seemed an eternity, the chief of police stood and walked up the aisle to where his brother was sitting, and stood before him. 'Brother,' he said to him, as his brother walked out into the aisle, 'I am sorry the way I have treated you. My conscience is killing me for not telling you when mother died two weeks ago, and you found out after we had buried her. Can you ever forgive me?'

" 'I forgive you from the bottom of my heart,' the brother said. 'I know that mother is now happy because we have finally made our peace and are brothers again.' The two brothers who had not talked for many years embraced and cried uncontrollably.

"Seeing this touching scene, the rest of the congregation stood up and went to one another making peace. In a few minutes the whole congregation was in tears. Hatred and meanness of many lifetimes were released as peace and love finally returned to the community. And God was glad his Son rose from the dead that day."

THE PARABLE
OF THE WOMAN ON THE
JOURNEY FAR AWAY

AFTER SERVICES one Sunday morning, while the people were having coffee and doughnuts during the social hour, two women were discussing their differing views on the meaning of the Eucharist. Some said it was merely symbolic, others held it was really Jesus. Unable to agree, they approached Joshua, who was standing nearby talking to a small group of people. "Joshua," one of the women asked, "what do you think of the Eucharist? Is it really Jesus or not?"

Joshua told them the following parable. "A woman was going away on a journey to a far-off land, leaving behind her best friends, whom she knew needed her very much. She thought long and hard as to what she could do to maintain the intimacy of these relationships. To give them a picture to remember her by would be a comfort but of little practical value. To leave behind such a symbolic memorial would be shallow and of little comfort. She finally decided to make it possible for her friends to communicate with her in a special way, so that, whenever they needed her, she would always be present to them.

"Eucharist is much more intimate, more intimate than God's presence throughout the universe, because Jesus makes himself present to each one personally in the Eucharist. It is sharing his inner life with those he loves, and being present in time of joy and in time of need. It is the most special gift Jesus could leave with my friends. To reduce it to a mere symbol makes Jesus appear shallow and superficial."

THE PARABLE
OF THE TWO PRIESTS

AT TIMES, people took offense at things Joshua said about the Church, so on a certain occasion, a priest said to him, "Joshua, you offend us. You are always criticizing the Church. You shame us and cause our enemies to rejoice."

Joshua responded, "I have never criticized the Church. It is the precious pearl Jesus talked about. It is Jesus' great gift to humanity. It is Jesus' living presence throughout history, but it is administered by human beings. Because the leaders are human they need constant reminders of Jesus' ideals for his Church. There were two priests totally dedicated to the Church. One loved his religion and faithfully followed all its laws without thought or question, even those which had far outlived their meaning, and were causing pain to many good people. Many of his parishioners kept the Church laws faithfully, while others lived in difficult and complicated circumstances, which made it well very difficult for them to live up to all the ideals demanded of them. The priest was insistent and unbending, because to him the Church was never wrong, and there was no excuse for not observing the law.

"The other priest also loved the Church, and kept its laws. But he spent his life meditating on the life of Jesus and Jesus' image as the Good Shepherd, who loved the sheep. He wanted to be like the Good Shepherd, continually searching for the lost, the troubled, the bruised and hurting sheep, so he could bring them back home. So often, however, when he brought them back home, they were mistreated and hurt even worse than before by inflexible priests and lay people who were more concerned about the law than they were about the pain in people's hearts. He thought often of the words of Jesus, 'The Sabbath was made for man and not man for the Sabbath, the law was made for man and not man for the law.' He realized only too well that the only Jesus whom many hurting people would ever know would be their pastors and priests, and important lay leaders. Rigid uncaring leaders were doing untold injustice to the Church by turning it into the Church of the scribes and Pharisees, intolerant and uncaring. Many Church laws were hundreds of years old and had little meaning in modern times, and were causing unnecessary damage to people. These laws had to change, but because so many officials and people were in love with the law and 'the traditions of the ancients,' as Jesus used to call them, nothing was being done. The priest spoke out loudly and clearly, and though he embarrassed and offended the leaders, they had to listen. In time, things changed. Now I ask you, which priest was more like the Good Shepherd and really loved the Church, the one who closed his eyes to all the hurting people and did nothing to ease their pain and alienation, or the priest who struggled to make the Church more faithful to Jesus' image of the Good Shepherd, and tried to bring the hurting sheep back home?"

THE PARABLE
OF THE TWO YOUNG MEN

A N ELDER in a community approached Joshua and told him of a young man whom he thought was having an improper relationship with a woman, which shocked the community, especially other young men, who were faithful in their observance of their religion.

Joshua, who knew well the human heart, told the elder the following parable. "There were two young men. One spent much time reciting long prayers and reading the Scriptures. He was always proper in his manners and exacting in his affairs. His companions were among those approved by his parents and church elders. He also contributed money to causes sponsored by their church.

"The other young man was a happy, carefree lad who loved life. He was not known for his interest in the Scriptures, though he was strongly drawn to Jesus. He enjoyed taking walks in quiet places, in the presence of God, listening to his voice in nature and in the beauty of creation. His open, friendly nature won for him many friends. He was especially close to those who were troubled or in pain, and spent much time with them, trying to comfort them and bring them peace. In his compassion he at times became attached, and entered relationships that were not acceptable to proper religious people. But, I tell you this young man was more pleasing to God than the other because his pure heart was filled with love of God and care for others, while the other was more concerned about his own righteousness."

THE PARABLE
OF THE STREET WOMAN

ONE DAY Joshua was introduced to several men and women who were widely respected in their community. They also occupied important positions in their churches. Joshua, however, could see their hearts and knew what others did not know. And he told the following parable.

"There was a young woman who earned her livelihood in a way that brought shame upon her family. Nice people shunned her company, and were ashamed to be seen with her, though many secretly took advantage of her services. Children made fun of her, calling her offensive names, when they saw her walking down the street. When she went to church, she sat in the back, and though the church was crowded, she always sat alone. Often her only prayer during Mass was the shame that rose from a broken heart. She never received Communion, because the only time she made a move to walk up the aisle, a woman looked at her with contempt and said, 'Don't you dare approach the Lord. You're a disgrace.' When the collection was taken, she folded up her gift so no one could see what she gave, but it was always much more than all the rest, and it was gladly accepted.

"The pastor knew the woman well, and whenever a family was in need, he called on this woman. Quietly and secretly, through the pastor, she cared for the family. As the woman had considerable resources, she was able to help many people in need, though no one knew from where the help came. Often she covered people's mortgages when they fell on hard times. She also made it possible for children of poor families to go to college.

"Knowing all the good the woman did, he asked her if she would do a reading at Mass. She felt honored, but was ashamed. 'Do not be ashamed. I know all the people in the parish and you are more worthy than most. Please do us the honor.' After much insistence she agreed. The following Sunday she got up to read. Whispers spread all across the church. After Mass the woman was ridiculed and taunted by the nice people. Only one little boy walked up to her and told her that she read beautifully, and hoped she would read every week. He became her only friend. All during the following week, mean and angry phone calls bombarded the rectory. Some even demanded the pastor's resignation. The bishop also called in the pastor and demanded an explanation. All the pastor said was 'I did only what Jesus did with the Samaritan woman at the well, and took to heart what he said about the woman in Simon the Pharisee's house: "Her sins, as many as they may be, are forgiven because she loves much." I consider that woman one of the holiest persons in my parish.' As the pastor stood his ground, the bishop ended by telling him to be prudent, as self-righteous parishioners could be very hateful and vindictive. They could destroy people and their reputations and feel no shame or guilt.

"The next week the woman declined the pastor's request for her to read, though she still went to Mass and sat quietly and alone in the last pew.

"Not long afterward, the woman died. Her body was found the following day after the pastor tried in vain to contact her. She had died in bed alone and of a broken heart, as she had no friends other than the little boy and the kind pastor who knew the hidden beauty in her soul. And although her life had changed many years before, no one but the pastor knew it, as people would never let her former reputation die. At the funeral, the church was empty, except for the pastor and one little boy.

"The following Sunday the pastor focused his sermon on the woman's life. He told the congregation at each Mass that the woman had long since changed her life. He also told them about all the needy people, some sitting in the church that day, who had received help through the years from the generosity of that lonely, broken woman who had died with only one friend, a little ten-year-old boy, who alone was present at her funeral.

"Many people left church that day filled with shame and guilt."

The Parable
of the Rich Man and the
Poor Man

PEOPLE WERE ASKING Joshua in what did true worship of God consist. Joshua said to them, "There were two men. One was very wealthy. The other was very poor. The rich man went to church frequently, was generous to his parish, directed his company's treasurer to give generously to church causes. He was also a highly trusted consultant to diocesan officials. His contributions to Vatican causes were well known. For this the Vatican showed its appreciation by granting personal papal audiences and the bestowal of papal knighthood.

"In his business, however, the man was known by associates to be unscrupulous, and miserly toward his employees. It was his custom, often at Christmastime, to lay off hundreds of longtime, dedicated employees to manipulate the value of his company's stock, then shortly afterward hire others at much lower pay. Because of their age, the employees laid off found it difficult to support their families and to keep their homes. Some even found themselves and their families in the streets among the ranks of the homeless. His companies were notorious for poisoning the environment and causing untold damage to people's health. The rich man was greatly admired, however, for his shrewd business genius, and was honored with prestigious awards by the financial community. He was recognized as a religious man, as his presence in church was duly admired by all. In truth, however, the man rarely prayed and hardly ever thought of God. His obsession was his business and the ever-rising value of his stocks. That was his true focus of worship, which consumed his whole life.

"The poor man, on the other hand, was not widely known nor honored for generous donations to prestigious causes, nor did he ever receive recognition for membership on important committees. He attended church, but sat off to the side, as he felt unworthy. His contributions were not great, though very generous considering his means. The clothes he wore were shabby, while he made sure his family was dressed with dignity. His meals were simple, often just soup and bread, so his wife and children could be well nourished. What little money he saved from work he shared with others less fortunate than himself. All day long his thoughts turned to God, not to ask for things but because he was touched by God's goodness, which he saw in creation, and he found peace in knowing he dwelt in the shelter of God's presence. Now, I ask you, which of these two truly worshiped God? And which of these two, do you think, has true dignity and nobility in God's eyes?"

THE PARABLE
OF THE GREAT LEADER

AT A TIME when civil wars were common, and people were killing and raping their neighbors, elected officials of the great world powers argued over whether they should send soldiers to protect the innocent and the helpless. Many argued that it was none of their business. "Let them kill each other. That is their problem, not ours. Why should our sons and daughters lose their lives to fight someone else's wars?" Others argued that it was only right to reach out and protect the helpless and the innocent. While others debated, the leader of an important country decided to send troops to stop the genocide. The debate, however, still raged on.

Two senators approached Joshua and posed the question to him, "Is there an obligation for a powerful country to jeopardize the lives of its own people to protect people fighting in another's war?" Joshua knew the question was not sincere, as he understood full well the issues of the debate. He told them the following parable. "There lived in a neighborhood a greatly feared and hateful bully. When children walking through the neighborhood encountered him, he beat them unmercifully, and left them lying half dead. Many eventually died. One day, a young man happened to be passing the same way and saw the bully beating a helpless child. He said to himself, 'It is none of my business,' and walked on. A short time later, another young man came by the same way and saw the bully kicking and beating a helpless child. He also walked by. Finally, another young man happened upon the scene and saw the bully battering other little children and felt compassion for the helpless children. He intervened to help the children and the bully turned on him. Although he was hurt, he drove the bully from the neighborhood forever. As the young man walked off, he was comforted by Jesus' words: 'Greater love than this no one has than to lay down one's life for others.' That command of Jesus applies as well to groups as it does to individuals. Do likewise if you wish God to continue blessing your country!"

THE PARABLE
OF THE FAITHFUL
NONBELIEVER

O NE DAY Joshua was with friends on a picnic outing.
Everyone was having a splendid time, enjoying the
food, the friendship, and the banter. There were some in
the group, however, who were not believers and had
never been baptized. One of the men spoke out: "Joshua,
our friend Jeff here has been a neighbor and a dear friend
to all of us. He is not Christian and has never been baptized. We would hate to think that when we all die, he
will not be able to come to heaven with us. Do you think
he will be able to go to heaven?"

Joshua looked at the man speaking and responded
with a mischievous smile, "So, you are all going to
heaven, are you?"

"Well, you know what I mean, Joshua. At least we

have a chance, as Jesus promised. But our friend has never been baptized, so what kind of a chance does *he* have?"

"Let me tell you a story. A mother had many children, all of whom she loved dearly. Some had magnificent talents and were highly respected. Others had different gifts that were also valuable. They put their talents to good use, each in varying degrees. There were others, however, who were not as richly gifted, and struggled much harder with the little they had just to survive the difficulties of life. Life was dark for them because they did not participate in the luxury the others enjoyed. They understood pain, and deprivation, and loneliness, and were like orphans because they did not possess all the resources of their brothers and sisters. One day the mother, who had grown very old and knew she was about to die, called in all the children. She distributed among them all her possessions. To the ones with many talents she gave gifts that were highly valued. To the others with different talents she also gave valuable gifts. But her kind heart went out to those not richly gifted during life, because they had received little all their lives, and what little they had they used to the best of their abilities in the struggle just to survive. To these she gave her most precious gifts. Their pain and struggling were a constant prayer for help and understanding that did not go unnoticed. The struggling in their lives was more touching to the mother's heart than the ease with which the others lived their lives.

"Just because God does not give everyone the gift of faith, it does not mean that God loves them any less. Good people before Jesus' coming were not baptized, and they are in heaven. Their lives, although without faith, preached many important messages, and though they may not have been blessed with all the spiritual gifts and comforts you have received, their good lives were an expression of their desire to please the God whom they did not know. Their lives without faith were empty and lonely, but unknowingly they performed a necessary role in my Father's plan. So, do not think that because you have been blessed with faith, others who have not been so blessed are less dear to my Father. Some are unknowingly very close to God, because their sighs continually cry out to my Father for light and understanding."

"So, what is the importance of baptism, then?" the man asked.

"It is important because it is a precious sharing in God's life while you are here on earth. It opens up for you the whole new world of God's life and faith, and gives added dimensions and greater vision to your life here on earth. Without these gifts, your lives would be empty and lonely and void of the consolation of knowing that God is your Father and that He loves you, and that his Son has redeemed you and opened for you the gates of heaven. That is of great comfort to you. Still, my Father has immense mercy and compassion for those who have been deprived of these blessings during their lifetime as they lived out a special message for him. However, mark my words, they will not go without their reward."

THE PARABLE
OF THE TWO DYING MEN

JOSHUA HAD JUST visited people who were suffering greatly. Two people in particular were still on his mind, when one of his companions said to him, "Joshua, what is faith? What can faith do for people like that who are in such misery? What is the purpose?"

Joshua answered them with the following story. There were two men who were suffering greatly from Lou Gehrig's disease. Little by little they were losing control of their muscles and had reached the point where they could not move their arms or legs and had to be fed, which was very difficult because the failing muscles in their throat made it a frightening experience. Both were home with their families, who took good care of them.

One man became more and more frightened by the

dreaded illness that was wasting away his body. All he could think of was his suffering and his fear, which he expressed in angry outbursts of rage and resentment that frightened those who tried to care for him, and even those who came to visit him. Often he cursed and swore over his unhappy lot and made life unbearable for everyone. He saw no good in what had happened to him, and welcomed the day when he would die. When he finally did die, his family were glad for him and, one might say, for themselves as well. Their only memories after his death were of his great anger and resentment. He left them no great spiritual heritage to inspire them in their own difficulties.

The other man accepted his illness with patience and great courage, and in his quiet way prayed frequently, asking God to help him and to bless his family for their love and devotion. Though he could hardly talk, he smiled his love and gratitude to all those who were kind to him. His ready smile reflected a deep inner peace, and his awareness that he would soon see God. His family and all who came to visit him were inspired by the man's serenity. Long after he died, the memory of his courage and joy still affected the lives of all who knew him, for he was a man of faith. Seeing the peace reflected in his eyes convinced his children that their father had a glimpse of a new and wonderful world waiting for him. They too learned to live for that world, where one day they could be reunited with him and all their other loved ones. For many years afterward people spoke of his great courage, his faith, and his peaceful smile as he approached his last days.

ANOTHER PARABLE
OF THE KINGDOM OF GOD

PEOPLE ARE always troubled with the kingdom of
God on earth. They would like to see the kingdom of
God on earth as perfect, without fault—as perfect as a divine presence. Jesus knew better. On one occasion when
newspapers were filled with articles about the shameful
behavior of some clergy, Joshua's friends asked him what
he thought of the articles and of the Church's reputation.
His response was simple and earthy. "The kingdom of
God is like a village a king designed as a safe haven for
people seeking refuge. He appointed good persons to ad-
minister the village and care for the refugees. He gave to
them the keys to the village and the power to guide and
protect the refugees, and guaranteed that the village
would be forever a safe harbor for people looking for asy-

lum from evil. As time went on the administrators appointed by the king died. New ones were chosen to take their place. Some were good people; some were bad and became administrators for their own personal reasons. They abused the people and caused many of the frightened refugees to leave the village. Most of the administrators, however, were good people and, in spite of unworthy administrators, the village will always be, as the king decreed, a sacred haven. And when the time comes, the unworthy leaders will be dealt with in the same manner in which they have treated others."

The Parable
of the Arrogant
Scientist

AS JOSHUA WAS TALKING about God to a group
of children one day, a proud young scientist was
standing nearby listening. He called out from the back of
the little group. "Holy man," he said with a cynical grin,
"why don't you tell them the truth, that scientists can create life and we don't need the nonsense of a god anymore." The children were shocked and turned and looked
at Joshua to see what he would say. Joshua was calm and
replied, "A scientist was making fun of God one day, and
said to him, 'God, simple people say that you created all
these things around us. But now we scientists can create
life, so you are no longer needed. We will one day control the whole universe. Then you will be totally irrele-
vant.'

"God smiled and said to him, 'When you can design and form a human eye and a human ear and synchronize the sight with the sound, then come to me and boast.'

" 'That may take time, but in time we will do that, too,' the scientist replied.

" 'Then the next time you see a person breathing her last breath, when the doctors say there is nothing medically wrong with the person, give back to that dying person her life.'

" 'I am sure that we will eventually be able to do that as well.'

"Unperturbed, God said to him, 'You seem quite sure of your genius to do almost anything that I can do.'

" 'There is no such thing as God; you are really an illusion simple people create to feel secure, because they are afraid of life and afraid of death.'

" 'Well, since you are dealing with an illusion, I am picking up all my illusions, all my stones and dirt and clay and dust. Then you must start where I started—with nothing. Now, show me how you will create a grain of dirt.' "

The children laughed as the young scientist blushed with embarrassment and walked away.

THE PARABLE
OF THE SUN AND THE LAKE

JOSHUA WAS SITTING in a park watching the swallows gliding across the lake in search of food. With him were men and women who believed in God, but were confused by the Christian idea of God. "Joshua," a thoughtful middle-aged woman said to him, "I believe there is a God, like the God the Jewish people believe in, and the God the Muslims worship. But the Christian God of three persons confuses me. How can God be one if God is three?"

Joshua smiled. "It is not easy to accept, and impossible for the human mind to comprehend because there is no other being like God. You continually think of God as an old, human grandfather. And if you look at God as a human, then you will surely be confused. Look at that lake.

It is calm as a mirror. See how beautifully it reflects the sun? That reflection you see, however, is not the globe in the heavens, yet the sun's presence you see there is real. It lights up the water and its heat warms the water, and causes life to grow. God is like the sun. But as his presence emanates from his being, it is not just a reflection. It is the image born of God's mind. Assuming a body it is called Jesus, the perfect reflection of God. Being God's image of himself, it contains all that there is in God, even his existence. That reflecting image of God also embodies God's love and, together with the Father, reaches out to the goodness they see in each other. That mutual love coming from the Father and the Son is the perfect giving of themselves, so perfect a gift it contains the essence of all that God is, but exists as a distinct identity. Jesus called that love the Holy Spirit, the love that emanates between the Father and the Son. The Son carried that love to God's creation, redeeming God's children and sharing God's life with all who choose to accept him. So, you see, because of the nature of God, God has to appear to humans as three distinct facets of his being."

The Parable
of the Two Gods

PEOPLE WHO DID NOT BELIEVE in Jesus posed this question to Joshua one day: "Why does Jesus demand acceptance of him as necessary for salvation? That appears to be narrow-minded and intolerant. The Eastern religions are more open-minded in their acceptance of other gods and make no demands on people's beliefs."

Joshua, with his usual composure, told the following parable. A talented woodcarver designed and fashioned thousands of wooden figures. He carved them with tender care and love, and spent hours every day making each one perfect, each special and different from all the others. One night the woodcarver had a dream. He saw that his great love for his creations made them all come alive. They looked at each other with awe and wonder. They looked at the woodcarver and said to him, "Who are you?"

"I am your maker, and if you follow where I lead, I will allow you to one day enter my world and become part of my family," he told them.

They laughed at him. They did not understand what he meant, because they never saw him make anything. They were afraid of him because he looked so big and so powerful. They did not feel comfortable near him.

The wooden figures walked off from the woodcarver to live their own separate lives. As time went on, they all noticed that some of their kind were far wiser and greater than the others. To these they began to show special honor and even began to worship them and ask them for special favors. They began to call them gods. The woodcarver became concerned because he was hoping they would love and accept him for all the love he had lavished on them. He tried to tell them that the gods they were worshiping were not real gods. But they could not understand, and insisted on worshiping their own gods. These gods could give them nothing, because they were gods that they themselves had fashioned. The woodcarver did not know what to do. All his pleading went unheeded and his wooden figures became angry with him and told him that he was mean and intolerant in not allowing them to worship whatever god they pleased. So he finally told them, "You may worship any god you please, but do not expect me to share my life with you when one day your life here comes to an end. Your gods may promise you, but they cannot give you another life, as they are not real.

They are gods you have created for yourselves because they please you."

The people who had asked Joshua the question were not pleased with his answer. "You also are reflecting Jesus' intolerant attitude toward other gods."

Joshua responded, "I am telling you what I know as truth. You have only one Creator and only he can promise you eternal life. You can choose to walk away from him, and worship gods of your own fashioning. You have the freedom to do that, but do not call your Creator names if you prevent him from sharing his love with you. Mark well my words! There can be only one God. A second god would limit God's being and his power and that is nonsense, as God cannot be limited or restricted in his being or in his omnipotence."

Those who questioned Joshua thanked him for his answer, and walked away deep in thought.

THE PARABLE
OF THE ARTIST

ONE DAY Joshua was attending a synagogue service. The rabbi, who was very close to Joshua, asked him to speak to his congregation and tell them what he thought God was like.

Joshua walked up into the sanctuary and, standing before the podium, addressed the congregation in these words: "One day a famous artist was asked to describe what he saw in a painting that was presented to him. The artist looked at the painting for a few moments and then said to those standing around, 'I see the soul of the painter. He is a man thirty years old. His mother died when he was a young boy. His father was very angry and was harsh and cruel toward him. The painter has seen much sorrow but has never become bitter or cynical. He has a kind and gentle spirit, and tries to bring happiness and joy to others through his art. He is, in a few words, a rare genius, but his talent will not be appreciated until he is long dead, because his paintings have such depth, it will take time, a long, long time, to discover their richness.'

"My dear friends, your rabbi, has asked me to tell you what I think about God. I will do more than that. I will tell you how you can come to know him. My Father is the Supreme Artist. The universe is his masterpiece. Scientists are trying to reach the frontiers of space. They will never find the frontiers of space. Even in that limitless space the universe reflects the Artist, infinite not only in his being but in the vast reach of his presence, throughout all creation, everywhere and at every moment. The painting of the universe is not like a painting on a canvas. It is more like a book, whose pages can be lifted up to reveal the artistic treasures of the past. If you could peel back the rocky layers of the earth, lying there on each page you would find evidence of life-forms far different from the plants and animals of today. Where did they come from? Was each created separately or did they evolve and unfold in the course of time? The manner is of little importance. The Artist's genius is revealed either way.

"Look across the world. It could have been designed flat and drab, with colorless life-supporting chemicals lying on the ground as food. But, no. There are mountains and hills and valleys and meadows and lakes and oceans, of exciting variety and dimension. And there are frogs and fish and lizards and birds, and animals of all sorts—each different, each unique, each reflecting something of the

Artist who designed them. Each has its own language, some in song, songs that thrill the heart and add music to the silent universe. And there is water, fresh, clear water, to drink and cleanse and comfort, and give life. And there are plants, millions of varieties, some strong and mighty in their size, others small and fragile in their delicacy. And look at the varieties of animals. The life-forms in creation are endless, each contributing to the life and growth and endurance of one another, all working together, all needing one another. And the food you eat. It could have been made tasteless. But the Artist had designed food with endless flavors and given to human creatures taste buds, so you could savor each of them with ecstatic delight. And he has given you eyes to see and ears to hear. And this picture is not silent. It speaks and it sings and it is happy and it is sad. It is alive, ever-changing, never the same, always in motion, never still. Each of these phenomena paints for you a smiling reflection of the face of God, and reveals to you the tender heart of an Omnipotent Creator.

"People have always been afraid of God. But can you not see, just from looking around you at all the love he has lavished on his creation, just for you, that he is a God who loves, a God who understands, because he made you as you are, not perfect, yet still beautiful in his eyes? And look at what he has given to you. Each day he gives, and each day he gives more and more, without count, without cost, asking nothing in return but that you use your gifts and resources to benefit the human family. And when you are learning to live and make foolish mistakes, often harmful to yourself and others, he does not condemn or flay you. He takes you gently by the hand and leads you to safety, often healing the harm you have caused others, protecting you from the fatal tragedy that could result from your blunders. So, do not be afraid of him. He loves you and thinks of you day and night. Draw close to him. He is ever by your side. He is your partner and your friend, who never condemns but patiently offers you endless options so you can grow as you learn from each faltering step you take through life. And one day he will bring you home to himself to be with all your loved ones. You have asked me what God is like. You see his image reflected daily in the world around you. It is an image of love and joy, of beauty and infinite tenderness."

THE PARABLE
OF THE FARMER AND THE
WILD BOARS

A NEWSPAPER ran a story about a well-known theologian teaching ideas that Church officials considered confusing and possibly damaging to people's faith. While having breakfast at a local diner, a man asked Joshua what he thought about the situation.

"Most people do not pay attention to theologians," he said. "It is a rare theologian who becomes well-known until he is censured. It is the attitudes of Church officials that concern people. There was a man who had a large farm with vast fields of wheat and corn. Occasionally, a few wild boars would wander around the edge of his fields and pick at the wheat and corn. As they never went deep into the fields, they did little harm to the crops. After grazing for a while, they would wander off without causing any trouble. The farmer watched them from his window and grew angry that they dared to feed on his crops. He could not sleep that night, nor the next night, nor the next night after that, but stayed awake planning how to rid his farm of the nuisance. The next time the boars came, he went out with a shotgun and tried to eliminate the nuisance. Frightened, the wild boars ran into the fields, trampling acre after acre of the precious crops. As the farmer was not a fast learner, it took him a long time to realize that he did more damage to his crops in a few days than the wild boars did in an entire summer."

THE PARABLE
OF THE TWO RABBIS

I T WAS SPRINGTIME, the season when young people in parishes are confirmed. However, one girl lived
far from the church and could not attend classes. She and
her parents offered to study at home and to do the re-
quired work. The coordinator of the program, however,
was very strict and refused to allow the girl to be confirmed if she did not attend the classes. The girl was very
upset, because she wanted more than anything to commit
her life to the Lord in confirmation. She was an unusual
girl. She prayed every day, and God was very real to her.
She was kind to other people and after school ran errands
for elderly people who had no one to look after them.
Faithfully every Sunday she went to church, even when
her parents did not go. If ever a young person was de-

serving to offer her heart to the Lord, it was this little girl.

People in the parish knew of the situation and were upset that the person in charge was so insensitive. They told Joshua the story and asked what he thought. He said, "There were once two rabbis who lived in the same village. One was a Pharisee, the other a kind and gentle man. The Pharisee had a sister who loved her temple but there was no place for her. People in another temple welcomed her and delighted in her gifts and accepted her into their community. Her brother the Pharisee was furious and would no longer have anything to do with his sister. The other rabbi, however, knew of the situation, and even though the woman was going to another temple, he knew where her heart was, so he always welcomed her into his home and allowed her to take part in their Shabbat service. The woman was so thrilled that this rabbi was kind to her, she started coming to his house every Sabbath for the Shabbat service. It brought back so many memories of childhood and the beautiful times at home when she was a child. Deep down, her heart was with her memories. Not long afterward, she went back to the temple, not the one where her brother was but the one where the gentle rabbi presided.

"A caring shepherd who loves his sheep will always be attentive to their needs; as the needs of the sheep are many and varied, they cannot all be treated the same."

THE PARABLE
OF THE UNWANTED CHILD

EVERYONE STRUGGLES, in varying degrees, with feelings of inadequacy. Many feel they are of little or no worth. Unpleasant childhood experiences often condition them to think this way. Sometimes, it is the result of individuals comparing themselves to others and assuming that others have been more blessed with great talent and they themselves have little that is of value. One day as Joshua was walking through a park, and people were walking along with him, a young lady named Anna said to him, "Joshua, I know that you have keen insight into human nature and understand people in a way that no one else can. I am deeply troubled. I have three brothers and a sister. They are all very intelligent and gifted in so many ways. I have no talent at all. What is my purpose in life? I don't seem to have any reason for being here, and I get so depressed."

"Anna," Joshua began, "you are judging talent the way humans judge talent. My Father does not judge people based on their talents. You must always remember that my Father created you for something very special, for something that only you and no one else can do for him. God has given you all you need to do that special work.

"Let me tell you a little story. Many years ago a girl was born to a very wealthy family. The baby was born greatly deformed. The parents were ashamed and humiliated that they should have such a child and wanted no one to know of it. It happened that in a nearby village there lived a poor couple who could have no children. They had hoped for a child all their lives but had none. The rich family sent an emissary to ask the poor people if they would like a child. The emissary told them the child was badly deformed. 'That makes no difference,' the poor couple replied. 'It is still a child that we could love and care for. We would be happy to take the child.' With that the emissary went back and told the rich man and his wife. They then delivered the unfortunate girl to the poor people, who were thrilled to have the child.

"They loved the girl and cared for her with extraordinary tenderness. They taught her to read and helped her develop her mind. Each day they spent hours reading to her and teaching her. As the girl was unable to walk or do anything with her hands, she made up for these handicaps by developing her mind. Her memory was extraordinary.

When she learned something she never forgot it. Her ability to understand people and events, her insight into people's lives, was unlike anything the people in the village had ever experienced. Word of this young girl's brilliant mind came to the attention of the king, who lived in the great city not very far away. He sent messengers to ask the parents if the young lady could be brought to the palace so the king could meet her. The parents were happy to please the king so they brought their daughter to visit him. When the king met the young lady, he was deeply impressed and asked if she could stay in the palace as his adviser. The parents were concerned about who would care for her. The king told them, 'You may come and live in the palace. Then you could care for all her needs.' The parents were very happy with the king's suggestion and they readily agreed.

"For many years afterward, the young lady served as the king's trusted counselor. When her real parents heard what had happened, they were beside themselves with envy and bitterness at seeing their daughter and the poor stepparents surrounded with honor in the palace with the king.

"So, you see, Anna, you may not have the same kind of talents as your brothers and sister. But God has given you gifts far more valuable than the gifts he has given to others in your family. These gifts you must find and nurture, so you can one day touch others' lives and accomplish the purpose for which my Father placed you here on earth. Everyone whom my Father creates has a purpose, though the world may judge them useless and of no value."

When Joshua finished, the young girl had tears in her eyes over the thought that she too was special to God and had something special to do for God.

THE PARABLE
OF THE WISE RICH MAN

THE WAR had broken out in Eastern Europe. The shocking spectacle of Christians killing one another was detestable. People were wondering what God thought about such senseless slaughter, so one day as Joshua was at a picnic with his friends, a man asked him what God thought of war. Joshua thought hard for a moment, then replied, "There was a wise and wealthy man who ransomed a kingdom of slaves. Each slave was purchased at a very high price and then set free. The wise man took great pains to understand each freed slave and his or her special talents, so he could provide work that would be not only productive for his own plans but that would give enjoyment and satisfaction to each one.

"For a long time the freed slaves were happy, but after

a while some became restless. They sowed discontent in the minds of others, and soon large, hostile groups sprung up, some grateful to the wise man, others angry and rebellious because they wanted power. They started a conflict that eventually involved all the freed slaves. Thousands died on both sides. Ultimately, nobody won, but the anger and suspicion and discontent became part of daily living among the freed slaves. Now you ask how God feels about war, which creates such chaos and destroys the lives of his children, whom he redeemed at such a great price, and for whom he planned a wonderful future in his kingdom. I tell you, those responsible for such havoc in my Father's kingdom will pay a heavy price when the time of settlement comes. Those who start such wars will pay the heaviest price. Those who could have made peace, but did not, will not be acquitted of guilt. Those who train evil men to kill the innocent struggling for justice will search in vain for excuses on the day of judgment."

THE PARABLE
OF THE SELF-RIGHTEOUS
MAN

ONE SUNDAY as Joshua was leaving church with his friends, one of them said to him, "Why do you go to church? Are you not above church?" Joshua's response was simple: "My family is gathered there. Why should I not be with them?" He then went on to say, "The building is of no importance. What is important are your relationships with one another. There was a man who considered himself righteous and ridiculed those who went to church, saying, 'I do not need to go to church. I can worship God from the rocking chair on my porch as I watch the hypocrites walk by on their way to church.' I tell you, he is the hypocrite. He cuts himself off from his brothers and sisters who recognize they are sinners and their need for God, while he sits smugly looking down on those whom he considers beneath him. My Father turns his back on that man's prayers, for he glorifies himself and not God."

Then Joshua went on to develop his thought. "My Father created people as a family, intending that they share relationships with one another. One cannot be holy all by himself or by herself. If one becomes holy it is only by loving and caring for others and accepting others' love and care. Holiness is in the perfecting of one's love for others. It is not just smugly avoiding evil. A person can spend his or her whole life avoiding evil, and still never do one good deed for another human being. I tell you, there is no room in heaven for such a person, because that person has never learned to love. It is love that bonds the soul to God, and that bond inspires love and care for others. In that alone is true holiness. Everything else is counterfeit. When I shared with the apostles my teachings, what I shared with them was relationships, my relationships with my Father and with the Holy Spirit. They are my family. I did not share a theological concept. I shared my family, who love all of you and care for you always with a love you will never be able to understand. I tried to teach the apostles, and all those who follow me, to look upon one another as brothers and sisters, and to feel the joy and pain of one another, and share one another's joys and sorrows. My Father takes delight when he sees his children gathering to pray to him. He knows they approach him with shame and guilt. He does not turn his back on them, for he knows that is part of being human. But, he wants them to worship him as a family, imperfect as that family may be. And he listens to their prayers, as imperfect as they may be."

The question was then raised by a woman in the group: "Joshua, you talk about relationships. Why are they important to you?"

"Joan, it is for relationships my Father created people, so they could share the richness of their lives with one another. You were not created to live for yourselves. You were created for one another. You are all related as members of one family. That is why it is important for people to develop relationships. God knows relationships are not easy because everyone thinks and speaks and acts from different experiences. A good relationship is a lifetime's work, but for those who have the patience to nurture a relationship, they will see how beautiful and rewarding it can be. That is the way my Father planned it, so everyone could learn to care for others, and in the process grow to become more like their heavenly Father. To the extent people mirror the heavenly Father's love and concern for others, to that extent they have grown in holiness. It is in perfecting your relationships that you become godlike. You cannot become truly holy all by yourself. Holiness is love. It is knowing and loving God and his creatures. That is why life's goal can be summed up in only one admonition: Love God and love one another. There can be no exception and no exclusion. When people think that all they have to do is keep commandments, that is wrong. Keeping the law is not a substitute for love. The law exists for those who have never learned to love and have to be told how to behave toward God and other human beings."

THE PARABLE
OF THE WOMAN AT THE WELL

JOSHUA'S DISCUSSING relationships that day gave rise to other questions of burning concern to people.

One was the issue of divorce and remarriage. "Joshua," a friend named Janet said, "you talk about relationships. What about marriage? Jesus said there can be no divorce. Practically half of today's marriages end in divorce. Are all those people sinners cut off from God?"

"Janet, my Father is wise and understanding. His laws are not arbitrary. They are for the benefit of his children. His laws are ideals for people to strive for. Marriage of a man and woman for a lifetime is a very high ideal. That ideal is necessary because the integrity of marriage is not for the benefit of individuals alone; it is for the good of society itself. The relationship between a man and a woman has been decreed not only by God but by nature and must be protected by society. There must be no substitute for or accommodation to the uniqueness of that relationship. Other human relationships, as beautiful as they may be, will never be the same as the bond between man and woman. It is the foundation of the human race.

"And yet, although it is sacred, God is realistic. He knows the human heart, and he understands that some relationships are not healthy and are destructive. And though it is counter to the ideal, God knows that people involved in those relationships cannot live together. It does not mean that they are evil. Remember the story of the woman at the well in the Gospels. She had been married five times, and in her last relationship was not even married. Jesus did not approve of what she did, but he accepted that she had been married five times. It is significant that Jesus did not chastise that woman as he did those he met on other occasions. He could still see goodness beneath the surface of her life, so he chose her to introduce the good news to the people in her village. Very few people measure up to all the ideals Jesus sets before them, so religious leaders must be prudent in the way they judge people, and in the way they treat those they glibly call sinners."

THE PARABLE
OF THE ANTS

J ANET, continuing on the same theme, asked him, "You say marriage is not easy; how can people maintain healthy relationships in marriage? People struggle day after day. Married life often seems impossible. Living together for a lifetime can be overwhelming."

"Janet, did you ever watch a colony of ants? Each ant has its own work to perform. As many as they are, you never see them fighting among themselves. They respect the differences built into each of them, and their daily work flows smoothly. Though it is instinct that drives them to be that way, still the same can apply to humans. Human beings are much more complex, and it takes many years for those in love to understand and appreciate each other. It takes even longer for a husband and wife to accept the differences in their personalities, and to respect those differences, and then an even longer time to enjoy them. But it is those differences that not only make the relationship an ongoing adventure, but also expand the possibilities for endless creativity and enjoyment in the life of the family. If they work as a loving team, they inspire each other to ever-greater creativity. The key is in focusing not on your own needs, but on understanding each other's needs, and the needs of the children, and trying quietly and unselfishly to respond to those needs. At the same time it is important to talk to each other when needs are not met. They should not be allowed to go unattended. That is dangerous.

"My Father intended married life to be a blessing and a joy. I know it is not easy. It was not intended to be easy, for love is like mining for diamonds. Its beauty and richness is unearthed only after perseverance and hard work unlock its secrets, and lay bare its hidden treasures. Unfortunately, too few have the patience and perseverance to keep their love alive long enough to find the treasure they have in their love. Hurt feelings nursed over a long time smother the soft glow of love's delicate flame. Understanding and forgiveness keep it bright. And the realization that only God can fulfill the deepest needs of the human heart will help husbands and wives not to expect from each other more than they can give."

ANOTHER PARABLE
OF THE RICH MAN AND THE
POOR MAN

JOSHUA," one of his friends said to him one day, "why do you always hang around with poor people?"

Joshua laughed and replied quite simply, "Probably because they are not as busy as rich people and have more time to spend with me."

"But you still seem to be more comfortable with poor people. Everyone notices it."

"Michael, you have to put yourself in God's place. God is like a mother of a big family. One son grew up to become a very rich man. He spent days and nights working at his business, which grew into a vast empire. He controlled many people's lives and treated them like the machines in his factories or the commodities he sold. They meant nothing to him. When he fired them they were often left homeless and their families with no support. Yet he went to church every Sunday. It was good public relations for his business. His time at prayer was spent planning business deals. He was highly honored by church officials and was given private audiences with the highest church dignitaries, who delighted in his friendship. When that man prays, do you think God enjoys listening to him? God has a heart, you know, and he has keen insight as well.

"God also was aware of the plight of the rest of the rich man's family. He knew the rich man rarely had time to visit his mother and father. Others in the family did quite well in their lives, except for a brother and a sister. One brother was losing his home because he could not afford the mortgage when the fuel costs soared. The sister was having trouble with her health and a difficult time raising her three children. This brother and sister were on the phone with their mother every day, concerned about her and her health, and eager for a word of encouragement from her lips. The rich son rarely called his mother. She would not see him for months on end, though her heart ached just to hear his voice. With which of these children do you think the mother spent most of her time? Remember, God is no different. And when the time comes, which ones, do you think, will have the places of honor in my Father's house?"

THE PARABLE
OF THE HEART'S DESIRE

WHILE ON THE SUBJECT of rich and poor, which was a preoccupation with Joshua, he told the following parable. There was a man who loved money and dreamed day and night about accumulating a large fortune. After many years he accomplished his goal. He had earned, by clever investments, billions of dollars. But, as he had few friends and many adversaries, he trusted no one and eventually was afraid even to keep his money in banks. He secretly excavated a large cave and reinforced it with concrete and steel doors controlled by electronic devices that only he could work. He would spend hours each day holding the gold coins in his hands and letting them slide through his fingers. The sound they made as they fell back into the chest of coins thrilled his heart. He had accomplished his life's dream. All during his long life, he never thought of God. There was no room and not enough time for that. Besides, he felt he did not need him. He was doing well enough without him.

One day, as he was in his cave counting his money, he had violent pains in his heart. Collapsing on his chest of gold coins, he was unable to reach for the electronic control that would open the door to let him out to call for help. And there he died alone and with the only god he ever knew, his gold.

There was also a kind and pious priest who prayed humbly and simply to God each day. He wanted more than anything to die peacefully when his time came. This priest would pray to Joseph each day that God would bless him too with a happy death the way Joseph died in the arms of Jesus and Mary. His prayers were always simple, the kind God likes, because they are said with such humility. As the priest grew old, he was often sick. One day when it was his turn for office duty in the parish, all the other priests were out for the day. At noon, the old priest collapsed. At the same time a beggar rang the front doorbell to talk to a priest. The housekeeper opened the door and told the beggar to sit in the office until the priest came down. When the priest didn't answer his phone, the housekeeper went upstairs and found him lying on the floor, dying. Running downstairs to call the hospital, she saw that another priest had returned momentarily to pick up something he had forgotten. She told him that the priest had collapsed and was dying. The priest went upstairs and, kneeling, lifted the dying priest's head and rested it in his lap, then prayed with him, heard his simple confession, and anointed him. The pious priest then went home, where he also found his treasure, the presence of God. When the housekeeper went back to the office, where she had told the beggar to wait, there was no one there.

Joshua said, "The moral is: Where your treasure is when you die, there will you spend your eternity."

THE PARABLE
OF THE PRIEST AND
THE DERELICT

WALKING DOWN a big-city street with a group of companions one day, Joshua noticed humanity's outcasts lying along the sidewalk. He looked at them with pain. One of his companions remarked, "Why don't the cops clean up the streets and get rid of all these bums. They contaminate the atmosphere."

Joshua ignored the remark and continued smiling at each one as he passed. Noticing one derelict in particular, Joshua paused, bent down, and whispered to the man, "Son, courage! Be of good heart! You have much to accomplish."

The man looked up with a blank stare, said nothing, just stared as one of Joshua's companions urged him to ignore the lazy, worthless outcasts and hurry past them.

Joshua again ignored the remark, and continued to smile at each wretched soul as he walked on. The pain in his heart was reflected in the sadness in his eyes and the anguished look on his face. Noticing how deeply affected Joshua was by what he saw, one of the men asked him, "Joshua, what do you see in these worthless dregs of humanity?"

"I see their pain, their loneliness, and the good that they can still accomplish. Only love and care can heal their pain and unlock the goodness frozen deep within. I will tell you a real-life parable. One day a priest was walking down a street strewn with people like we just passed. The priest nodded to each one as he passed and stopped to smile and say a kind word to one of them. His companions were annoyed that he delayed so long. He ignored their comments and continued on.

"Many years later, the priest received an invitation to a graduation at a famous university, with the urgent request that he attend. When the time came, the priest drove to the graduation. Receiving a copy of the ceremony and scanning the list of those receiving their degree of doctor of medicine, he did not recognize any of them. As one by one the recipients proceeded to the stage to receive their diploma, the priest seemed not to recognize any of them. Then, one of the graduates, after receiving his diploma, walked to the microphone and briefly told the story of why he was there.

"'One day,' he started, 'when I was lying in a gutter on a New York street, in the depths of despair, a group of young men walked by. With them was a young priest who smiled at each of us derelicts lying along the sidewalk. He stopped and whispered a kind word to me, telling me I had a great future ahead of me and that many people needed me. I was deeply moved that a priest saw good in me. I prayed that night for the first time in years, and decided the next day to change my life. The struggle was long and difficult, as no one wanted me. I was alone and had no money, no clothes, no home, and nowhere to go. But gradually I found a menial job, and slowly climbed back into life. Later I applied to the medical school and, to my surprise, was accepted. Today, with great joy in my heart and gratitude to God, I hold with pride my medical diploma. I would like the priest who had faith in me to please stand if he is in the audience.' The priest did not know whom he meant until the young doctor called out his name. Embarrassed, he stood up as the audience applauded. Afterward, the priest asked him how he knew him. 'The young men with you that day were wearing sport jackets with the school's name on them. I called and finally found what priest was out with them that day.' "

Joshua said, "So you ask what I see in those people lying along the sidewalk. I see my Father's children, broken in spirit and without hope. A kind word or a warm smile has changed many a life on the edge of despair."

THE PARABLE
OF THE ARK

QUESTIONS concerning the kingdom came up frequently among the people who followed Joshua. One day, a disgruntled man came up to Joshua and said to him, "Joshua, the way I see it, the Church has long since departed from the ideals Jesus taught long ago. I gave up on the Church and now I practice my own religion. What do you think of that?"

Joshua looked at the man, and saw the pain he had suffered at the hands of Church people, and said to the crowd standing around, "Do not expect the Church to be like God or to be like heaven. It is not like God. It is not like heaven. It is like Noah's ark, floating here and there on troubled waters. Only, its safety is assured. It will always be filled from top to bottom with good and bad.

There will be troubled people among the leaders as well as among the sheep. Do you think the people living in Noah's ark found it pleasant? Yet, it was their only hope. The Church is like the ark, and even when the experience is not pleasant, the Church will still fulfill the purpose for which Jesus established it. To abandon it is to abandon the ark. It is neither wise nor safe. The Church is God's gift and he will never abandon it. Nor is there a substitute that can ensure Jesus' promises. Substitutes may provide a pleasant experience here, but not the eternal assurances Jesus gave his Church."

THE PARABLE
OF THE HUSBAND AND WIFE

ONE DAY after a television program about the devil and diabolical possession, a young teenage girl named Janice approached Joshua and said to him, "I saw on TV last night a movie about the devil. It was scary. All during the movie I wondered if the devil was real or just a movie character or a figure invented by clergy. Joshua, what do you think of the devil? Is the devil real?"

"Janice, evil is real. It does not come from God. It comes from the hearts of men and women. The devil you talk about is not a human. He was the brightest of all God's angels, who would admit of no one greater than himself. Banished from heaven, he spends eternity defying God by seducing humans into evil. What the devil wants more than anything is to capture the minds of God's children. He knows he can never win their hearts, but he *can* take possession of their minds. This he does by casting fear into people, which many clergy exploit by talking incessantly about evil and the ever-present power of Satan. They thus play into Satan's hands by fastening their people's minds continually on Satan rather than on God.

"There was a woman who was deeply in love with her husband. Her whole life centered around him. When he was away from home, her heart ached for his presence. Since she was very beautiful, men were captivated by her beauty and her intelligence, and tried to distract her from the love of her husband. No one, however, was able to succeed. There was one man who realized that it was impossible to win the woman's heart. So, he set about befriending her friends, causing them to talk continually about him to her, about his brilliance, his wisdom, his shrewd business mind. The woman became curious, and began thinking more and more, and even to dream about, this man she had never met. The more she thought of him, the less she thought of her husband. This constant preoccupation led to a curiosity to meet him. Her husband saw the change and their relationship slowly waned until they drifted so far apart that there was nothing left. This also is Satan's strategy. He shrewdly seduces God's friends into carrying out his evil plan by focusing people's attention on himself and away from God, until their thoughts are centered more on himself than on God. That gives Satan great delight."

The Parable
of the Mosquito

ONE DAY, while Joshua was sitting around a camp-fire with some friends, a mosquito bit one of them. The person swatted the insect and immediately asked Joshua why God created such nuisances. Joshua laughed loudly and then replied, "Remember, Jonathan, my Father is not a bore. He is a playful God, and the Master Artist. He loves to create. He did not create the mosquito to bite you. He created the mosquito for itself, so it could enjoy its life. It is designed with incredible engineering precision. Remember, my Father likes to create and give life. It is the same with all the animals of the past. They don't have to have a purpose that benefits humans. Their purpose is merely to enjoy being alive. Did you ever watch an artist work? You wonder what in the world the artist is creating. It often seems to make no sense. But to the artist it does, because it is coming from the artist's mind. It is an idea or a fantasy the artist wants to make real. Often it is just for the sake of creating something different or special that an artist paints or sculpts something. It need not have a useful purpose. Just for it to exist is reason enough. It is the same with God. God just enjoys creating, giving life to something that does not yet exist, for the sole reason that it can enjoy being alive. Sometimes my Father creates odd and funny things merely to make his children laugh. Remember, my Father is not a bore. He is a playful God, and a God of joy. You often take life more seriously than God does. If you understood that, it would explain a lot, and make a big difference in your life."

"Are you saying God creates individual creatures?" Jonathan asked.

"Some he does, others he merely guides through their development as nature unfolds. Either way, they are his handiwork. God is very subtle and efficient in the way he works. Placing a blueprint within creation allows his creation to be always the same while ever unfolding into new wonders. Every now and then, he may alter a genetic code to fashion a new creation. Scientists will look for a link, but will never find it, because it is new. That is what my Father did with man. Scientists will find similarities, but never the real link, because there is none."

THE PARABLE
OF THE DOCTORS

I T WAS ELECTION TIME, and people were talking
about politics and politicians and political parties and
different forms of government. It was only natural that
someone would bring up the subject with Joshua at some
time or other. It was a subject Joshua never brought up in
conversation, probably for the same reason many people
prefer not to discuss it, except with those who share similar views. On this occasion, a man said to Joshua, "Do
you think that God's law should be the basic code of law
for our country?"

Joshua did not even have to think about it. He answered as if it was a subject he had pondered for a long
time, and was ready with his response. "In an ideal world
it would be so, because my Father's law is for his children's

benefit. However, you do not live in an ideal world and people have many different beliefs and have to try things out until they find what works. My Father never imposed his law on the world but gave it as a gift. He respects people's freedom to choose. Here you have a country where people are free. Just as my Father does not impose his law on everyone, so a government of free people has no right to impose God's law on its citizens. Religious leaders have a responsibility to teach their people to understand and appreciate God's law and to love God's law. When they do that, the people's good moral sense will be reflected in the country's laws. When the clergy fail in doing that, it is not right for the Church to use government to force on people what they themselves have failed in teaching. Worship of God and respect for his creation must come freely from within, not imposed by the state. The state in a free society must respect the decisions of its people."

"Do you think, then, that a free society is a good thing if God's law is not enforced?" the man asked.

"A free society is the only society that properly respects the freedom God gave his children. It is the responsibility of clergy and parents to instill love of God and a proper sense of right and wrong in people. Then those people will either be responsive to what is important to God, or they will refuse to listen. If they refuse to listen, then they will have to learn through sad and painful experience, like difficult children, that *their* way has brought nothing but disaster upon them. If they do listen to sound religious leaders, then you have a proper balance, where the state reflects what the people believe and, where there are differences, people will learn to respect those differences. God himself tolerates many things that he may not approve. The state can do no more. Only in a theocratic society can God's law be promulgated and enforced. But then the state and religion only too easily become God. And that is worse.

"I notice in medicine that there are different approaches to healing, and different medical doctrines. One school of doctors feels that their approach is the right one and those who have been taught differently are wrong. Doctors in another school believe the opposite. If a medical center is to work efficiently, both must learn to respect each other and work together for the benefit of the patients, otherwise there will be chaos, as both groups spend their lives fighting each other to the good of no one and to everyone's detriment. That is what can happen if people are uncomfortable living in a free society and insist that God's law be promulgated and enforced."

THE PARABLE
OF THE HONORABLE
BUSINESSMAN

ONE DAY at a party, Joshua and his friends were talking about their work and various ventures they had
undertaken. Though Joshua was not involved in business
he enjoyed listening to his friends discuss how they conducted their own affairs. Things they shared with each
other seemed innocent enough, but to Joshua they were
disturbing because their approaches revealed a side of their
personalities that he found less than noble. A young man
named John was telling the others how he was able to in-
crease his business by fifty percent in two years. "Of
course," he said, "I could not have done this without a
good friend whom I embarrassed into selling me necessary
components at cost."

"That's one way of doing it," another man, named

Mickey, interjected, "if you're lucky enough to have a friend like that. As for me, I meet my contacts for lunch. We discuss our projects over a few drinks, work out deals that benefit everyone involved, and a few days later sign the contracts. It's fun; we have a good time, and, of course, the bottom line is it's good for business."

"Well, that sounds simple enough," added another man called Paul. "I have to meet my clients after hours for late-night dinners, spending whole evenings away from my family, discussing plans and programs. Afterward, I still don't know whether I made an impression. Sometimes I don't find out until weeks later whether they even understood what I was talking about. These high-tech things are so new to old-time executives, it's like speaking a foreign language. Kids understand it better."

"Joshua," Mickey injected, "you're very quiet. What do you think of all this earthly stuff we humans are involved in?"

"Not being in your kind of business, it's all rather new to me. When it comes to friends, I always take friends seriously and value their friendship. When I grew up, people did business pretty much the way you do business now. People don't change very much. But one man stands out in my memory very clearly. He was a good businessman and very successful. He had many friends because other businessmen knew they could trust him. His company's products were always of the highest quality. One trait that was remarkable about him was the way he treated his friends. He would do business with them because he wanted to help his friends in their businesses. His friends appreciated that because their other friends used them. And though his business was a large operation, which grew steadily, his family always came first, and everyone in the family knew that they were more important than anything else. Besides that, the whole town admired and respected him."

"Well, I guess that's a real-life parable, Joshua, we could all benefit from," John said. "I certainly would enjoy doing business with somebody like that."

"There are many people who would like to be like that, but somebody has to begin the change."

THE PARABLE
OF THE TWO BUSINESSMEN

"JOSHUA, you always have a unique perspective on everything. Tell us about business," Jonathan said.

"Business is nobody's calling in life. It is necessary for individuals' survival and for people to help others along the way. People in business, however, have many occasions to do good or create havoc with people's lives. There were two businesspeople. One man worked hard to get ahead in his company, which was one of the greatest in the country. He was intelligent and shrewd. He made all the right moves and had the ability to make others whose good work threatened his advancement look incompetent and untrustworthy. Little by little he eliminated all his competition, anyone who could jeopardize his advancement in the company. His fellow workers knew him to be ruthless and ambitious, but his superiors saw him as loyal, progressive, and dependable.

"So, he was promoted from one position to another until he finally became the company's top executive. He soon began buying up other companies and put together a huge conglomerate, as you call them. To make these combined companies work efficiently, he fired tens of thousands of loyal workers who had dedicated their lives to the company. It made little difference to him. At the same time he took multimillion-dollar increases in his own salary. He was now famous, and businesspeople everywhere, who were like him, sought his advice and counsel. He was their hero. All along his path he left lives ruined by the poverty and homelessness he forced upon them. For him this was just good business. People were to him like the products his company manufactured: If they were not needed, he disposed of them. And thus he disposed of people's lives.

"Though people thought his business moves were shrewd, they secretly despised him for his ruthless insensitivity to the lives of his workers. In time he moved to a prestigious community on the coast and bought a huge mansion befitting his greatness. When he tried to join the area tennis club the members rejected his application, because no one wanted to associate with him. But when the club fell into financial difficulties, they were forced to accept him as a member when he bought the entire club outright. From then on they had to tolerate him. When he eventually retired from his high office, he was a very lonely man and not long afterward he died.

"The second businessperson, a woman, came from a poor family. She, too, rose through the ranks of the company she worked for. Because she was bright and efficient, she was rapidly promoted. However, in each department where she worked she noticed and appreciated the abilities of other workers and recommended those with talent for better positions, and people with families for better-paying situations. She also allowed the workers to make recommendations that could improve the company, and rewarded those who did so. Workers of integrity loved her. In time she too rose to the top position in the company and in shrewd economic moves bought out other companies. She knew the workforce then had to be reduced because of overlapping jobs. However, unwilling to destroy people's lives, she appointed a committee to help her solve the problem in a way that was just and compassionate. The committee recommended that she offer early retirement to a large number, and then set up a job-placement office to find suitable employment elsewhere for the others. Those for whom she could not find jobs she treated most nobly. She took a vast reduction in her own salary, so they could stay on until they found work elsewhere. When other top company officials saw what she had done, they followed her example. The monumental transition was accomplished without destroying one life or one family.

"Both these people eventually died. When they appear before God, what do you think God will say to them, and how do you think he will judge each of them? To my Father it is not how much money you make or how great you are in this world that counts, but how much money you gave away and how compassionate you were to those in need."

When Joshua finished the parable, his friends were silent. "Joshua," Mickey said, "you force us to search our souls. Your vision is so clear and your heart is so true."

"Now that you see clearly, follow with true hearts what is now so clear."

THE PARABLE
OF THE TWO BROTHERS

ONE DAY a deacon who worked in a prison asked
Joshua if he would come and visit with the inmates.
Joshua agreed. After obtaining all the necessary permis-
sions, the deacon conducted Joshua on a tour of the insti-
tution. When Joshua saw the conditions in which the
prisoners spent most of their lives, he was visibly shaken,
but said nothing. He spoke a few words to each of the inmates as he passed their cells. What he said was simple but
contained much food for thought. Each one felt Joshua
knew his whole life story, especially when he talked about
the terrible things they had done, and the rage that had
brought them to such a sorry plight. They also knew he
himself could feel their loneliness and abandonment. He
also told them that if they accepted their imprisonment

with a proper spirit, it would go far in atoning for the wrong they had done. He encouraged them all to pray each day for those they had unjustly injured.

The deacon then took Joshua to a large meeting room where he had previously arranged for a group of inmates to meet with Joshua, so he could speak to them. There were about sixty-five men in all, bearing various criminal records ranging from homicide to armed robbery, physical and sexual assault to lesser crimes. Two guards were standing in the back of the room watching over the men, seated in rows before a table in the front of the room, with two chairs for Joshua and the deacon.

The deacon introduced Joshua, who then rose to speak to the men. What he said was brief. He told them a parable that none of them would ever forget. "Men, I understand full well why each of you is here. I know that two of you are innocent of what you have been unjustly convicted. Jesus was also unjustly convicted, and said nothing. He did that for you. Bear with that injustice patiently and with courage. You will be well rewarded by my Father for the freedom that has been unjustly taken from you. Have hope. In not too long a time you will be freed.

"I would like to tell you all a story. There were two brothers. The older brother was very shrewd in things of the world. His parents were proud of him and sent him to the best schools. The younger brother was not as bright, but had a gentle spirit. He tried hard to win his parents' approval, but no matter what he did, he could never measure up to his brother, with whom he was always being compared. As time went on, the older brother excelled in school and won awards for high achievement. The younger brother eventually dropped out of school and fell in with troubled youths, who created havoc in their neighborhood. After many warnings they were arrested and sent to prison. In their shame over their younger son's behavior, the parents renounced him and refused to help him. 'He brought it all on himself,' his father said, 'let him pay the price for his stupidity. I don't want to have anything more to do with him.' Though the mother pleaded with the father, he forbade her to contact him in any way.

"In prison the younger son became withdrawn and spent much time locked in his cell thinking. He knew he would spend many years there before his release. During that time no one ever came to visit him. His older brother was ashamed of him and would never admit he had a brother. It would be bad for his image, especially as a highly respected public figure. His younger brother was still proud of his older brother and prayed for him every morning and every night, asking God to help his brother achieve his dreams. Strangely enough, in prison, the younger brother changed completely. He had no family who cared for him. He had nothing to prove to anyone any longer. For the first time in his life, his real self began to grow. He was kind to the other prisoners, but was close to no one. When coarse and unsavory characters tried to antagonize him, or seduce him, he ignored them, which made them harass him even more. But, the young man had grown strong within and refused to be drawn into conflict.

"There were on the prison staff sadistic guards who enjoyed mentally torturing the inmates. These men enjoyed enraging the prisoners, then putting them into solitary confinement, or depriving them of privileges, for becoming belligerent. No matter how hard these guards tried to antagonize him and incite him to anger, he would never give them the satisfaction of giving in. One day one of the guards who tried to make life so difficult for him entered his cell and asked him why he was so different from the other prisoners. He pulled aside a towel hanging on the wall, and etched on the wall was a crucifix. 'That's why,' the young man said. 'I have nothing anymore, no family, no possessions; he is all I have. I think about him and the way he lived, and the way he died, and I know he is always with me. He is my only friend, and I am determined to make him proud of me.'

" 'When the other prisoners aggravate you, don't you want to punch them out?' the guard asked.

" 'No, they're troubled and I feel sorry for them. I know I am strong and it would be easy to fight, but for what? I pray for them because I know life is not easy in here for them. I have at least found peace. They haven't.'

" 'Do you pray for me, too,' the guard asked, 'even though I am mean to you?'

" 'Yes, every day.'

"From that day on the two men became friends and the guard would bring him news clippings about his brother, who was rising high in the political world.

"The younger brother saved every one of the clippings, and read them over and over. He knew politics bore many perils, and he worried that his brother might make mistakes and ruin his carrer. Strangely enough, he was never envious of him. He prayed hard that God would help his brother succeed in everything he did. He made a pact with God that if he would protect his brother, he would try hard to live a holy life, even if he was a criminal. He knew God listened to him. He often wrote letters to his brother telling him how proud he was of him. The letters were never answered, but the younger brother continued to write.

"Years went by. Daily routine in the prison never changed. But life among the inmates changed, and all because of that one young man, whose gentle goodness touched the lives of all the others. One day he was found dead in his cell, of a heart broken for want of love. The whole prison mourned for days, but his memory continued to inspire them. Many earned early release because of the change in their lives.

"The older brother had in his lifetime acquired great fame, of which his parents were very proud. In time they all died. In heaven, to their surprise, they saw their younger son. He had a place of great honor and dignity, and was widely respected by those near to God. 'We don't understand,' the older brother and the parents complained. 'He was a criminal. How did he get such a high place here, when we have nothing?' And God said to them, 'You did well on earth because your younger son became a saint in that lonely prison, and spent his life praying for you. His unselfish life was filled with goodness. His only friend was my Son. Now you can see how close he is to my Son. You, on the other hand, lived paltry, selfish lives, which were of little value to me. You are here now because your brother, and your son, from his loneliness and his abandonment prayed so earnestly for you. Even though you showed him no compassion on earth, *he* always loved *you.'* "

THE PARABLE
OF THE CROWDED BUS

ONE DAY Joshua was sitting in the lounge waiting to be interviewed on a national television program. Joshua was dressed ordinarily. The racial characteristics of his features, however, were always difficult to define, though his complexion tended to be more light than dark. In the small lounge with him, also waiting to be interviewed, were two well-known black religious leaders, one whom his companion called Joseph, the other a professor at Harvard. Joshua tried several times to engage in friendly conversation. Each time he was answered with just a quick remark, as the men ignored him and continued with their own conversation. Though Joshua was never really shocked by what he found in human nature, he was surprised to receive this kind of treatment from men who had a national reputation for fighting bigotry and racial hatred. Finally, after his third attempt not just to be civil but to really show that he was interested in their lives and their work had failed, Joshua decided that he had to make a statement.

"Gentlemen," he said, "I have sat in this room for twenty-five minutes with you and you have refused to show me the slightest token of courtesy. I have something I would like to say to you. I know your reputation as leaders concerned about racial prejudice. What you have demonstrated here in the past half hour is the very thing that you publicly condemn. I would like to tell you a little story. I was on a crowded bus one day in Washington. When the bus stopped at the next corner, a very large white woman carrying heavy bags full of groceries got on the bus. A black boy, no older than ten or eleven, was sitting nearby. He saw the exhausted woman and had compassion for her. He stood up and offered his seat to the woman. She thanked him profusely. The boy's companions, however, were angry with him for giving his seat to a white person, and when they left the bus a few blocks later, they started fighting with him. I tell you, gentlemen, there was more courage and nobility of soul in that little boy than in many who pose as champions of justice, while hiding their own bigotry and hatred under the guise of concern for the poor. Which of those boys would you have been, had you been there on that day?"

The two men seethed with anger that Joshua had laid bare their hypocrisy.

THE PARABLE
OF THE MOVIEMAKERS

IT WAS THE DAY AFTER a young teenager had gone
berserk and killed many of his schoolmates. The question was brought up to Joshua as to who was at fault.
Some were blaming the tragedy on television and the
movies for glamorizing crime. "Joshua, what do you say.
Are the movies to blame?"

"Not many years ago," Joshua said, "a young movie
producer was inspired by a friend to produce good movies
to help raise the moral tone in the country. After much
discussion, he followed his friend's advice and began to
produce movies that were not only inspiring but also very
popular. Besides that, they won many awards. Many
young people were affected by those movies, and told
later on how they had changed their lives. Now there are

movie producers whose heroes acquire high-powered ri-
fles and semiautomatic weapons, and destroy all those who
oppose them, and show contempt for human life. Young
children acquire the same kinds of weapons and murder
those who oppose them. If there are people who claim
their lives were inspired and changed for the good by their
movie heroes, how can movie producers today claim that
their insane heroes have no effect on the impressionable
minds of many children who already suffer from emo-
tional problems? Does it not seem obvious that evil and
insane behavior made attractive will appeal to already
troubled minds? Young children would not engage in
horrible massacres unless they had seen them repeatedly
laid out before them as attractive."

THE PARABLE
OF THE GOOD PASTOR

JOSHUA HAD a reputation for favoring priests and other clergy who were known to have personal problems, while shunning those of impeccable reputation for the exact observance of the law and religious traditions. At a house party one day, a man who was very close to his religion told Joshua that he was offended by Joshua's attitude toward good, observant clergy. "Rather than shun these good men, you should hold them up for our admiration," he said to Joshua.

Joshua looked at him for a brief moment, then said, "In the days of old there were the same kinds of clergy as there are today. There were those who were in love with the laws and the old traditions, and there were those who saw the law and the traditions in a different light, often as hurting people. I will tell you a story. There were two young priests who had been friends for many years. One was named Paul, the other John. When first ordained they worked together in a large city parish. In parishes there are many people whose lives wander far from religious ideals, for various reasons, some personal, some beyond their control. When these people came with problems to the two priests, each treated them differently. Paul saw them as unfaithful to Church laws, and insisted that they observe the laws first before he could arrange for them to receive the Church's blessings.

"John, on the other hand, sat down with them and asked them to share with him their experiences and why they had wandered so far from their Church. In most cases there were painful situations in their lives that were very difficult to resolve, but they did the best they could under the circumstances. John showed compassion and tried to do what he thought Jesus might do in the same situation, acting accordingly, which usually meant bending the law. One day, a young girl approached John and asked if she could enter the Church. John listened to her as she told her story. She was nineteen years old. She had become pregnant over a year before and her parents and her closest friends insisted she have an abortion. She refused because she did not want to take the life of her baby. Her boyfriend also wanted her to have the baby. The girl did not marry the boy because she did not know whether they really loved each other enough. They waited. Months after the baby was born, they married. Now, the girl wanted to come into the Church. John gladly made arrangements for her to take instructions, classes for which she had attended regularly for over a year. A week before Easter, when she was to be baptized, Paul found out that the girl had not been married in the Church. He forbade her to present herself for baptism. Deeply upset, she asked John what she should do. The two priests argued vehemently over the matter. John appealed to the chancery and the girl was allowed to receive baptism.

"Shortly afterward, Paul was made pastor. He became more insistent than ever on the rigid observance of rules and traditions. Though the people liked the way he conducted the Sunday services, and found him to be friendly at social gatherings, they rarely came to him with personal problems, however, or approached him to learn about God or their religion. They were afraid of his kind of religion. In fact, many left the church because of his inflexible attitudes. John, however, was never made pastor. People still flocked to him, not only with their problems, but to learn about God and Jesus' teachings. He was a kind and good shepherd who reached out to the troubled, bruised, and hurting sheep and, like Jesus, picked them up, placed them on his shoulders, and gently carried them back home, where he fed them. Now, I ask you, if you were Jesus, to which priest would you feel close?"

THE PARABLE
OF THE UNJUST FATHER

O NE DAY as Joshua and his friends were walking
along the avenue in a bustling metropolitan city, they
came across a group of religious people picketing the
headquarters of a large corporation. The company had a
reputation for unjust treatment of employees and the ex-
ploitation of workers in poor countries. As they approached the crowd, some on the fringe came over to
them and asked if they wanted to join in the picketing.
One of the picketers recognized Joshua and asked him
what he thought of their campaign against injustice.

"It is commendable," Joshua said, "but there is much
work to be done in the family."

"What do you mean?" the person asked, rather hurt.

"There was once a very large and powerful family, not

just one family but many families that formed a large, extended community. It was a good family, dedicated to God, and did much good for humanity. But there were many problems in the family, which the members did not recognize because things had always been that way. The father ruled the family strictly and with absolute authority. Even the grown-up children, many of whom were well educated, were not allowed to think for themselves but had to think exactly as their father told them, and do always as he instructed. When he decreed something, no one was allowed to discuss the matter any further, not even the adults. Of course, it was, he thought, his way of protecting all these grown-up people. Anyone who dared to think for himself or express thoughts different from his was considered disloyal and ungrateful, and had to be punished.

"The women in the family were treated like servants, who had to do as they were told and be subservient to the men in the family. Although some of the women had managed to become well educated, they were allowed to assume only subordinate positions, positions always dominated by the men, who also had to be totally submissive to the demands of the father. As a result, no one in the family grew up or matured, as they were never allowed to think for themselves or live a life independently of their father and his favorites, who controlled every aspect of the life of the family. The father's inner circle were responsible for much of the oppression. They would not even allow their brothers to marry. When one did, he was expelled from the family.

"As a result of this unhealthy repression, the family became dysfunctional, and its members could not become real, healthy people. They often manifested their repression by giving vent to angry feelings toward others, especially toward those who disagreed with them. Even people friendly to them often thought them strange and difficult to understand, and almost impossible to work with. Enduring such injustice for so long, the family failed to recognize the unjust way they treated people, though they were sensitive to cruelty and injustice in other places. So they started crusades to fight for peace and justice far and wide. One of the brothers, however, was struck one day when he finally realized that much of the injustice they were fighting against ultimately had its roots in their own family, as they influenced so much of the society around them. One day, at a gathering of his brothers and sisters, he spoke out and said to them, 'Do you not realize that the very injustice we are fighting against has its roots right within our own family? We never recognized it, because we have been living with it all our lives. It is our family who has the greatest effect on the society around us. People look to us for leadership and ideals. So, if we want to make a difference and fight injustice in the world outside, we must first start here at home. I know it takes more courage to fight injustice at home than it does to fight injustice in faraway places, but that is where we have to start if we want to really change the world.' When the father heard what his son had said, he was furious and expelled him from the family and ordered the rest of the family to have nothing more to do with this disloyal and rebellious son. Cut off from all family support and cast outside, it was impossible for the young man to survive. A short time later he died, abandoned and alone, forsaken by a family famous for its preaching of justice, compassion, and love for others."

would help them. As a result, she had many students in her class. To accommodate them the principal assigned a large room for her use. The first thing the teacher did was learn about the family background of each of the children so she could understand them better. As the children were upset so frequently, she decided never to send a child to the principal's office, but to solve the problem in the classroom. The children appreciated that. She also realized that the school curriculum was designed for students who would one day go to college. Students with good academic ability did well. Students with less ability often failed or did poorly. They were ashamed, as they knew the other students looked down upon them as stupid.

"The teacher realized that the school was doing severe damage to these children, and to their self-respect, by forcing them to take courses in which they could not achieve. She decided to test the children for abilities other than academic. She was surprised to find that many of the students had extraordinary talent for art, mechanics, music, carpentry, languages, electronics, and computers. So, the teacher approached friends at local industries and asked if they would be willing to help her with these students. It was just an experiment, she told them, but she was convinced it would have a wonderful effect on the students. Her friends were only too glad to help her. They brought to her class electronic equipment, computers, art supplies, and an old automobile that one of the men owned. They managed to find musical instruments that people were no longer using. Some of the men and women at various facilities even obtained permission from their superiors to spend time at the school teaching these students.

"In a short time the change in the students' behavior was remarkable. They came to school early to start work, whether it was electronics, or computing, or music, or art, or mechanics. By the end of the year, those students with little academic ability had made remarkable progress. There was no more disturbing behavior in class, no more discontent or noisy outbursts. The students were happy and filled with enthusiasm. They now knew they had abilities, and were proud of what they had accomplished. All year long there was not one incident of crime or drug use. The students were too excited over what they were doing and felt a new sense of self-worth.

"Children need to be loved. When they know they are loved, their lives change. Putting young children in prison is a mindless attempt to rid society of a problem, something politicians do only too easily; like Pontius Pilate, they wash their hands of the problem and sell their souls to please the crowds. Their judgment will be harsh when they plead for understanding on Judgment Day, as will the judgment of those who execute rather than heal those whom my Father created with infinite love."

THE PARABLE
OF THE PATIENT

THE NEWS MEDIA were filled with items about the possibility of war. People were curious as to Joshua's opinions about war. As he watched the news with friends one evening, the question was posed to him, "Joshua, what do you think of war?" The answer was quick in coming.

"War is the nearest thing on earth to hell. It is evil. My Father took such pains to create each of his children with infinitely tender love, and to see them slaughtered like animals is the greatest offense against not just humanity, but against God himself. There is never a justification for starting a war."

"What does one do, then, when a war starts, just stand by and watch?"

"Wars are always instigated by a few whose hearts are filled with evil. When a doctor examines a patient and finds that there is a cancer just beginning to grow, he does not bombard the whole body with powerful weapons, for fear of destroying the whole body. He will define the area, target the source, and, with a laser, render it harmless."

"Do you mean that someone should assassinate those who start a war?"

"I did not say to kill them, but if they should die in an attempt to isolate them, that is not assassination."

"But how does one do such a thing?"

"It is difficult, but human ingenuity always achieves what it knows it must accomplish."

THE PARABLE
OF THE FAITHFUL WORKERS
AND THE EVIL WORKERS

ONE EVENING a news announcement told of a mother of a large family whose husband was killed in a plane crash while he was on a business trip. Those watching the television with Joshua knew the family and were very upset at hearing the news. One of them said to Joshua, "Why do bad people always prosper while good people have so much tragedy?"

"That is not always true," Joshua responded. "There are many good people who do quite well in their lives. And there are many evil people who are plagued with tragedy. But you must not judge by what you see. Life here is only a small part of human existence. Life transcends far beyond this life, which is just a passing-through. Let me tell you a little story. Suppose there was a rich man of vast wealth who had great dreams of things he wanted to accomplish. He also had at his disposal a large number of workers. These workers he sent out, each with a special assignment, to many and varied circumstances.

"Some of his workers were honest people, while others turned to evil ways. The honest ones carried out their master's assignment efficiently, while the others schemed to better themselves and cared little for the work the master assigned to them. Some of them prospered, as did some of the good workers. However, the good workers were more concerned about accomplishing their master's assignment and did not gain riches for themselves.

"Finally, the time came for them to return and report to their master. The master's assistant read out the accomplishments of the honest workers. The master was impressed. 'Well done, honest ones! You have well earned your reward. Enter into my domain and live in my presence forever, for you have been faithful in carrying out the work I assigned to you. I know some of you have suffered much in your lifetime in fulfilling the work I gave you. Now you will be close by my side, with special honor in my domain.'

"Then the master's assistant read what the evil ones had accomplished. It was indeed very little, and the master was angry. When the evil workers saw their master's anger, they tried to make excuses. 'But we became very wealthy and important in the life we spent there,' the evil ones replied.

" 'The wealth you gained there was of no use to me. I would have been more honored had you been generous to those in need, but you kept all for yourselves. The assignment I gave you to accomplish, you did not accomplish, and now you come back to me with empty hands. You did nothing to deserve a place in my family.'

" 'But where shall we go? There is nothing in the darkness outside,' they pleaded with him.

" 'You have your friends with whom you carried on your business. Perhaps they will still befriend you.'

" 'But they are no better off than we are. Is there no place for us here?'

" 'You have forfeited your place in my domain. There is now no place but in the darkness outside.'

"So, the evil workers departed from the master's presence, while the honest workers enjoyed the happiness and pleasure of being among his family."

THE PARABLE
OF GOD IN PRISON

ONE SUNDAY after Joshua's friends had returned home from church, they met Joshua at lunch. Before long they began complaining about the way the priest said Mass.

"What did he do that bothered you?" Joshua asked them.

"He's old. We can't understand what he says. His sermons are boring."

When they finished complaining, a woman said that the service she went to was so delightful. The priest said Mass in Latin, the music was beautiful; it was just like what she remembered as a child.

When they finished, Joshua looked at each of them and said, "Not many years ago, in a concentration camp, a guard smuggled some bread and wine from his supper to a priest, a prisoner in the camp, then left. The priest gathered a few of his fellow prisoners around him and, trying to remember as best he could the prayers, he offered Mass. There were no vestments, no singing, not even Scripture reading. There was no sermon, as there was no time. The room was freezing. They closed their eyes and reflected in their hearts on the presence of the loving God who had come to visit them in the freezing-cold barracks where they knew they would soon die. Though there was nothing pleasing to the eye or to the ear, the men's hearts were filled with gratitude. I tell you, that simple Mass was more beautiful than any Mass said in a cathedral, where people leave saying how nice the Latin was, and how nice the singing was, and how eloquent the sermon delivered by the nice young priest. Those in the prison were happy because God was with them. They cared little about the trappings. Those who are concerned about the trappings rarely think of the God who has come to visit them, but spend their time being entertained or finding fault afterward because there was nothing that pleased them. One wonders whether it is really love of God and gratitude that inspire them to come to worship."

THE PARABLE
OF THE COMPLEX MACHINE

A CONCERN of many people has been the differences between Scripture and science. A young college student told Joshua one day that her minister strongly advised her to drop her science course as it would undermine her faith. "Joshua," she said to him, "I respect your opinion very much. What do you think of science? Can it contradict and damage my faith?"

"Janice, if the teacher is a good scientist and teaches scientific facts accurately, he can say nothing that could threaten your faith, because there is nothing that a scientist finds in God's creation that could contradict what God has revealed in Scripture. Science can be the handmaiden of Scripture in helping people to understand what God has revealed. Scripture is not a catalog of scientific facts. It is a record of God's love for his children told in a simple way for people who knew nothing of science. To look there for a scientific account of nature is ridiculous. So, what scientists find in nature complements and clarifies what is contained in revelation.

"A man bought a complex machine. With it was a user's manual explaining how it worked, with directions for its operation, but with no explanation of how it was originally designed. After a long time, the owner began to have problems with the machine until it no longer worked. Knowing nothing about those matters, he hired an expert to take the machine apart and find what was wrong so he could restore it to good working condition. The expert then explained to the owner, since he was a curious man, all the inner workings of the machine and the purpose of each part. The owner then for the first time understood fully the meaning of the operating instructions in the manual, because he now understood how the machine was put together, and how each part worked. The expert's explanation did not contradict what was in the manual. It merely clarified it. It is the same with the relationship between God's revelation and science."

The young girl was very pleased with the way Joshua helped her to understand and resolve what had become for her such a difficult problem.

THE PARABLE
OF THE WOUNDED FAMILY

EACH YEAR Christians of various denominations celebrate their symbolic flirting with unity. In some places clergy take it seriously, and going farther than just symbolic gestures, they take bold steps to draw closer to one another. In other areas it is just a nice ceremony, which gathers people of different beliefs into a prayerful and well-intentioned service of worship of our common Father. Many thoughtful Christians who take seriously Jesus' prayer for unity at the Last Supper are concerned that the churches talk about unity, but in reality do so many things that make unity more and more difficult to attain.

Frustrated with all the talk and no forward movement, a man approached Joshua one day and bluntly asked him, "Joshua, you are not afraid to speak your mind. What do you think of all the divisions in religion? Jesus prayed for unity. How should Christians respond to Jesus' plea for harmony among his followers?"

Joshua thought for a moment, then said, "Jesus is not pleased with his followers preaching different versions of his message. Truth was important to Jesus, as is the integrity of his message today. Each group gave up a part of that message when the family was torn apart. When they are willing to humble themselves and lay aside those things that separate them from one another and reclaim what they have given up, then they will fulfill the will of God. That takes honesty and great personal integrity and a willingness to lay aside many things they treasured from childhood. If the father of a family is severe and wounds his children until they wander off and become strangers, the only way the wounds can be healed is if the father is willing to humble himself and respect the rights of those who remained loyal and then, with humility and love, invite the others back home. Then, those who come back home are not compromising and returning to what they have left but to a family cleansed and healed."

"Joshua, what are you saying?"

"Jesus' followers gave up too much when they left the family. They must reclaim what they lost, as well as their rightful place in the family. And Peter, who is still with the family, must become one with the other apostles, and remember that Jesus appointed and gave authority to twelve apostles, not one."

THE PARABLE
OF THE TWO HOLY MEN

A NEWS ANNOUNCEMENT told the story of two
men who wanted to marry. Naturally, Joshua's friends
could not wait to ask him what he thought of it. "Do you
think it is a good thing, Joshua?" a woman asked him.

"Human love in sex," Joshua replied, "is a sacred responsibility as well as a gift. Sex was not decreed by civil
law. Nature designed male and female for a practical purpose, to assure the continuation of the human race. And
the love of man and woman is the tender bond that pro-
vides security to the family. Nature's design was efficient
and practical, as well as comforting. And there is no substitute. Any attempt to mimic that relationship is not authentic and no human authority can make it authentic. If
society attempts to do so, he is merely endorsing an illu-

sion, and does no real good for those for whom it is intended."

"Is it wrong, then, for such to love each other?" the woman continued.

"It is never wrong to love. To love properly takes discipline. For those whose love is different, discipline is even more important, because the pain and danger to themselves and society is so great. God's law is not a cruel law. It is to protect his children from hurt and tragedy. Though people do not understand, God understands and is compassionate.

"I will tell you a beautiful story. There were two men, both highly gifted, which was what my Father intended, because he had a special mission that only they could accomplish for him. These two men loved each other with a deep and holy love. They always knew there was something special about the bond that held them close. Though they would never have children, God planned that they would still be able to create. Both of the men were well-trained artists, and wanted to do something that would not only be an expression of their love for each other, but, more important, of their love for God. They decided to design a park with exquisite gardens. The money for this park would not come from other people's donations, but from their own personal earnings. It was a genuine work of love.

"As the work progressed, visitors saw appearing streams and ponds and waterfalls, and gardens with flowers and shrubs of every kind. Placed discreetly throughout the park were delicately carved sculptures and figures, which one of the men with his own hands had fashioned. Each of these carvings and stone sculptures suggested, in an attractive and subtle way, the presence of God in every turn of the path through the trees and shrubs and gardens. When the park was finished and opened to the public, people of all types came to enjoy the beautiful creation of these two men. In time, thousands of visitors meditated and found peace in the holy presence that hovered over that sacred place. When the two men died many years later, people flocked from far and near to honor their memory, and their love that had brought so many strangers closer to God. Let each one who hears heed what he hears."

THE PARABLE
OF THE TWO MONEYLENDERS

DEEP IN THEIR HEARTS, most people hunger for spiritual things, but in their lives they face so many material problems that it is difficult for them to make the transition into spiritual values. One of the gnawing problems so many poor people face is their lack of money for necessities, and their inability to borrow money. This question came up one day as Joshua was invited to speak at a luncheon attended by a party of banking officials in the area.

In his talk Joshua spoke with urgency about the great human potential that lies untapped in neighborhoods written off as unproductive. After the talk, a bank president spoke out and said banking people would like to help the poor, but they were bad risks. To which

Joshua responded calmly, "I am aware of the losses that banks incur because of the high percentage of unpaid debts. I wonder if those debts are owed by the poor. We know that they are not. I will tell you a story, a true story. There were two moneylenders. One was the president of a large and prestigious bank whose policy it was to lend out money to the solid businesses and to those whom the community respected as honorable, and, of course, to close friends. During a period of staggering interest rates, many of these businesses and a high number of honorable citizens defaulted on their loans, and the bank had to be taken over by another bank.

"The other moneylender, together with a group of well-intentioned friends, decided to open a bank to help the poor embark on their own business ventures. At first they loaned out small sums to people widely respected in the neighborhood who had solid ideas for a new business. They also provided advisors to guide them along the way. At first, the businesses operated out of people's homes in a small and modest way. As they paid back their loans, they were allowed to borrow more money, which made it possible to expand their businesses slightly. In the course of a short time, the moneylenders enabled over five thousand poor people to begin their own business. It was not long before the bank became the largest bank in the country, with assets far beyond what anyone could have imagined, working with the poor. The return rate on their loans, even at the time of high interest, was over ninety-seven percent. The little bank flourished. The venerable old bank, suffering great losses from the defaults of its prestigious clients and highly placed friends, was bought out and lost its identity."

The Parable
of the Corrupt Union
Official

A GROUP OF MEN were coming home from a nearby factory as Joshua walked past. Some of the men recognized him and greeted him. Not far away, two union officials were walking toward them. When the two groups met, they exchanged greetings. Some of the workers introduced the union leaders to Joshua. They were well dressed and very proud-looking. These officials did not ordinarily socialize with the workers, from whose ranks they had come, but with the socially elite. Since they had become important, the workers rarely saw them except at election time.

"I am glad you take the workers' side when you told that parable about the chairman of the corporation a while back," one of the union leaders said to him.

"More people should take the workers' side," Joshua said sarcastically. "I will tell another parable. There was a young man who worked in an automotive plant. He worked hard and the other men liked and respected him. When time came for the workers to elect officers for their union, they voted overwhelmingly for that young man. He did much good for the workers and was always fair to both workers and management. He won the respect of everyone. In time he was elected to high union office, and was able to win even more benefits for his men.

"Then he began to change. He was important now. He demanded a huge salary for himself, and benefits befitting his new position. He no longer associated with his workers. He was too important for them. His friends were the wealthy and influential people in society, of which he considered himself one. He went on expensive vacations, not with his old worker friends but with the rich and powerful. And he built a mansion for himself where he could throw parties for his rich friends.

"The men no longer respected him, but when they tried to elect someone else to take his place, he used dirty tricks to eliminate him. Even though the company had been treating the workers with considerable fairness, rather than trying to foster even better relations between the company officials and the workers, he found endless excuses to create conflict. Creating chaos and conflict was the way he kept his job.

"Realizing the situation had become impossible, the company gave up and began to send work elsewhere, laying off hundreds of workers in the home factories. Workers in one plant after another lost their jobs unnecessarily because of this greedy and corrupt union official and his lieutenants.

"There was no need for endless conflict. Shrewd and sensitive leaders could easily have worked to everyone's benefit. But power and greed poisoned the atmosphere, and everyone lost."

The union officials were furious at what Joshua had said, because they knew the workers understood that he was talking about them. Enraged, they turned and walked away. One of the workers said to him, "That was a good story, Joshua. You do understand our problems, don't you?"

THE PARABLE
OF THE WICKED JUDGE

ONE DAY a family from Korea came to Joshua to ask his help. "Joshua," the father said, "I have been told by the immigration judge that he does not like my papers and that I have forty-eight hours to leave the country with my family. I asked the judge what was wrong with my papers, and he would give me no answer. I told him my papers were all truthfully documented. He just told me that that was his decision. Joshua, I have two little babies and the trip, staying in jails across the country until we reach the West Coast, will be unbearable. Can you help us?"

"I will do what I can," Joshua promised.

The next day, Joshua went to the immigration office and asked to see the judge. It was impossible, he was told. But, through his insistence, the judge finally consented to see him, but only to give him a verbal lashing for being a nuisance. At which point Joshua told a story to the judge and the whole staff standing within hearing range. "There was a father and mother who had two babies, one hardly four months old. The father was summoned to court one day and, despite lack of any evidence of wrongdoing, was unjustly sentenced by the judge and his family ordered into a cruel exile. Many years later, the judge died and went before the Judge of all. When the Judge looked at the wicked judge's record, and saw that he was a man of no compassion, he said to the wicked judge, 'You stand before me asking to enter my kingdom, when you so mercilessly and unjustly denied good people entrance into your own country? Give an answer for your cruelty to others, for it is difficult to see why you should be allowed to enter my kingdom.' I tell you, mark my words, it will go hard for that judge on the day of judgment."

Joshua did manage to make it possible for the family to enter the neighboring country, and eventually to return and become citizens.

THE PARABLE
OF THE YEAST IN THE DOUGH

PEOPLE WERE COMPLAINING to Joshua one day that there was nothing for them to do in their parishes. One young man, who was very upset, said to him, "Joshua, Jesus talked about his disciples being yeast in the dough to change things around them. I went to my pastor and told him I had talents I wanted to put to good use in my church, and he told me they had all the talent they needed and there was nothing for me to do. How are we supposed to do what Jesus told us if no one wants us?"

Joshua smiled good-naturedly and told the boy, "There were no parishes in Jesus' day. Jesus' friends lived in a society that was evil and filled with injustice. Jesus came to raise the level of that society and mold it into a new creation filled with his spirit of love, forgiveness, and compassion, a just society where people would respect one another. Let me tell you a story. There was once a judge who also wanted to be of service to his parish. His pastor also told him that he knew of no way the parish could use him. Unoffended, the judge thought and prayed over what Jesus said about the yeast in the dough. He realized that he could not have meant that his followers should all work in the parish. They would be stepping all over one another. What Jesus meant was that each one should help to create a better society, a society fashioned after the mind of Jesus.

"The judge had a reputation for strict justice and had sentenced people to death and to long prison terms. He asked himself if Jesus were in his place, would he have treated people that way. The matter troubled him deeply. One night the judge had a dream. He dreamt that Jesus had taken his place as judge. Jesus was angry at the system of justice in the community, where people boasted of their Christian righteousness, and gave criminals their supposed just deserts. Jesus did not see them as loving people, but as vindictive, unforgiving, and self-righteous, like the Pharisees of old. He saw prisons as the anterooms to hell, animal cages unfit for God's children, and places devoid of love. He saw human execution as barbaric and an arrogant affront to God's authority over human life. When criminals came before him, his sentences were calculated to cure and to heal, not just the criminal but the community as well. Those who were not dangerous were sentenced to work for those they had injured, either by compensating them from their own income, or by doing work for the community. In this they were closely monitored. Those who had committed wicked crimes and were dangerous he banished from society to deserted places where they worked in factories and modern industries with others of their type. There they learned skills and trades and were paid just salaries, which were sent home to support their families and pay restitution to victims' families. People were sent in to talk to them and counsel them and prepare them to live in the world outside. The prison conditions were humane and therapeutic and fostered an atmosphere where even the most troubled souls could, over long periods of time, be healed.

"This dream had a profound effect on the judge, and he realized God was showing him the way to change that most barbaric part of society to reflect the mind and heart of Jesus. A Christian society must be radically different from a society devoid of Jesus' love and forgiveness. The judge found his role in the community and from that day on became a reflection of the justice and compassion of God to the community. His form of justice was his tribute to God, and did honor to Jesus' spirit. In time other judges, seeing the good that was accomplished, followed his example.

"Though you are not a judge, young man, you, too, can become a model to reflect God's goodness in the world. Go and be a light to your own little part of the world."

THE PARABLE
OF THE TROUBLED BOY

ONE DAY, as Joshua was walking past a schoolyard, he noticed children taunting a boy who was different from the rest. The boy was trying hard to hold back the tears as the others made sport of him and prevented him from walking away from them. Several teachers, standing at a distance, watched but did nothing.

Joshua walked over to the children and, as they ignored him, walked over to the boy and stood next to him. One of the children began to taunt Joshua, and the others chimed in, and laughed. Unoffended by their behavior, Joshua was determined, nonetheless, to teach them a lesson. "What if I should tell you some things about yourselves that no one else knows, how would you feel? What if I were to tell you that two of you wet the bed last night, and three others still suck their thumbs? And others who are afraid of the dark, and their mothers have to leave the light on when they go to bed so they will not be scared?" The children became strangely silent, but did not walk away. There was something about Joshua that held their attention.

The teachers standing by walked over to see what was going on. One of them asked Joshua who he was. When he said he was just walking by, the teacher told him, "Well, you better just keep walking."

"If you had been doing your job, I would not have had to come over. I remember when you were a lad, you used to show the same meanness to a lonely, frightened boy in *your* neighborhood, and sent him home crying every day. You were quite a bully in those days. Yes, I will leave, but before I do, I will tell you all a story."

The children gathered around, eager to hear the story.

"Not very long ago, there was a young boy whose parents were mean. They punished the boy for the slightest things he did wrong, and sent him to bed with severe hunger. The father often beat the boy and burned him with lighted cigarettes. Feeling unloved and unwanted, he became withdrawn and rarely talked. At school the children noticed he was different, and made fun of him, trying to provoke him into a fight. They laughed at him in front of girls, which filled him with shame and self-disgust.

"As time went on, the boy grew to hate not only the children at school, but his parents as well. He began to do strange things, first, so someone would notice his pain, then, convinced that no one cared, in desperation he committed crimes. The police arrested him and eventually the boy was sent to prison. Not long afterward, having lost all hope, he hung himself.

"Now, let me tell you what would have happened to that boy if someone had cared. His parents treated him the same, the children treated him the same, but there was a teacher who noticed his pain and went out of her way to befriend him. She was not just a friend, but like a mother to him. She saw that he was very bright and encouraged him. He was naturally a quiet boy and enjoyed science, so she encouraged him to do well, and promised that if he got good marks, she would arrange for him to attend college. As the years passed, he went to college, graduated, and continued learning. Eventually, he became a scientist and dedicated his life to research. Together with others, he found cures to several life-threatening diseases."

When Joshua finished the story, everyone was silent. Joshua walked toward the boy, took him aside, and spoke to him quietly, so no one else could hear. The boy thanked him, shook his hand, and walked away with a smile. The teachers turned and walked away, ashamed.

THE PARABLE
OF THE CRIPPLED IN MIND

JOSHUA WAS SPEAKING to a group in the park one day. A woman stood at the edge of the crowd, listening to every word. A sad look of pain and loneliness reflected her deep inner pain. Joshua's eyes kept moving back to her as if to reach out and touch her soul. She felt a peace she had never before experienced. Joshua had been responding to a question that a person had asked him, why some children are so good and some, even with the best of care, become troubled and stray.

"You cannot judge by what you see on the surface. The person you see is not the person whom God sees. The real person, you cannot see. The surface of a person's life hides from view a whole inner world that only God can see. You ask why a person makes bad decisions and does bad things. I am going to play tricks with you for a moment. Look at the person next to you. What do you see? Each one looks ordinary and friendly. Now turn and look again. What do you see? The person looks the same, but this time you see something different in the person. You see something malicious and evil, and you feel frightened. Angry feelings shoot up inside you, and you feel you have to protect yourself. Before, what you saw was normal. What you saw the second time was an abnormal perception. There are some people who live their whole lives like that, and see others as frightening and threatening. They see life through a distorted inner vision, which often leads them to do things that others look upon as evil, but that they judge to be reasonable.

"Now, close your eyes! You are in a supermarket. You have to buy food for your family, but you have no money. You see all kinds of things you know your family would enjoy. You pick up one item after another and put them into the shopping cart and try to find a way you can slip out of the store without being caught. You feel you have done nothing wrong. Your family is hungry and you have no food, and, since you have no money, you cannot afford to buy what you would like. You feel sorry that your family will never have nice things like other people. You tell yourself that everything belongs to God anyway, so you decide that there is nothing wrong with helping your family to live better. And you feel no guilt in taking all those things.

"Now, open your eyes! What do you feel? You feel shocked that you could have thought it was all right to do something so wrong. This thinking is normal and healthy. You are fortunate. There are some people for whom distorted thinking and acting seem reasonable. Their inner vision is not normal. It is not through any fault of theirs. Some persons are crippled physically, and you pity them. These people are crippled in their minds. People do not pity them. They are frightened of them and society punishes them severely, often locking them away in prison.

"But I see their pain and their inability to help themselves. They know they are crippled but have no way of helping themselves or even understanding what is wrong. It is impossible for them to explain to others what is wrong with them. They themselves do not know. They go through life frightened and lonely, because they have no hope of ever finding understanding or acceptance. So be kind in your judgment of others, and be grateful that God has blessed you to see clearly and to walk proudly. Do not judge and you will not be judged. You who see clearly will be judged because you see clearly and, in full knowledge, you make decisions that are often wrong. So, do not be quick to judge others as evil, because God sees into the heart and judges justly. Many who appear to others to be good, God sees their evil. Many who appear to others to be evil, God sees their good. In the judgment, many eyes will be opened."

After Joshua finished speaking, people asked him how he did what he did. He smiled and told them, "One day you will understand." Then, Joshua walked over to the woman standing at the edge of the crowd. The people were dispersing, and he was left alone with her.

"Thank you, Joshua, for all the things you said. I am one of those evil people. I am so frightened. I don't know what to do to help myself. Every day I do so many stupid things and get into so much trouble. I don't realize that they are stupid until afterward, when someone explains it to me. For a while I think I understand, but then I get confused all over again, and do the same things, or things just as bad. You really don't think God hates me, do you, Joshua?"

"No, God does not hate you. He is a kind and caring Father who loves you very much. He understands your pain. So, go in peace. From this moment you are healed. Be grateful for God's gift!"

The woman looked up into Joshua's eyes and, as the tears flowed down her cheeks, she threw her arms around him and whispered, "Thank you," and walked away.

THE PARABLE
OF THE VILLAGE
WITH NO MEN

THE NEWS MEDIA were filled with articles about women in business and women in the Church. Throughout Hebrew and most of Christian history, women were not admitted to official roles in worship or in decision making. In modern times, widespread questioning of this policy has generated great interest and emotion. So, it was only natural that one day someone would ask Joshua for his opinion. "Joshua, do you think Jesus would approve of women priests?" The woman who asked the question was not an activist but just concerned about the issue. "Jesus did not pick any women to be apostles," she added.

"You are right. Jesus did not choose women to be apostles. The idea was totally foreign to the religious customs at that time. Women were not even allowed to worship with their husbands, or to sit with them in the temple or the synagogue. It was considered improper for an Israelite man to even talk to a woman in public. Women had no legal standing in the community. A woman apostle would have been a pariah and subject to insult and rejection. However, Jesus did perform a very bold act one day, which contained a powerful message. He went into Samaritan territory and searched out a Samaritan woman. She had been married five times and he picked her to be the messenger of the good news to the village. She was truly an apostle to that village. Even though the townsfolk insulted her, they still had to come to see if what the woman told them about the Messiah visiting her was true."

"But, Joshua," the woman pressed him further, "you did not answer my question."

"I was telling you that Jesus was not opposed to women being apostles, just like Jesus was not opposed to married men being priests. In Jesus' eyes there is no distinction between man and woman in the work of the kingdom. Let me describe a situation for you. During a war, there was a village where all the men were sent off to faraway places. Only the old men and young boys were left. The women cared for the village. The church had no priest. There was no liturgy, no breaking of the bread, which was the most sacred gift of Jesus to his followers. I ask you, would a bishop be faithful to Jesus if he allowed those people to be deprived of the Eucharist, when he could anoint women to bring Jesus' presence to them?"

THE PARABLE
OF THE COAL AND THE
DIAMOND

J OSHUA," a man said, "why did Jesus not take away suffering when he came as the Messiah?"

"People grow through their suffering. A child who has never had difficulties to overcome, never grows up. He remains forever a child. Athletes subject themselves to torture to make their bodies fit to compete. Without it they would be unfit for the struggle. Their training is a small price to pay for victory, so they think nothing of it.

"In long suffering a person acquires patience. In struggling against dangerous opposition a person acquires courage and endurance. In struggling against personal weakness a person acquires understanding and compassion for others. God did something more important than take away suffering. He transformed it. Suffering is like a piece of coal that has been subjected to the intense pressures of the earth. After a long time all the impurities are burned out of that piece of coal and it is transformed into a price-less diamond. That is what happens to a person of faith who endures suffering with grace. Suffering bonds the soul to God, and will one day become the person's crown of glory. Suffering is a small price to pay for resurrection and eternal life."

The Parable
of the Blind Man

A MAN whose father had recently died was distraught not only over the death of his father, but because his father had no faith. "Joshua," the man said, "my father was a good man, and though he had no faith, he helped everyone. He often said how much he envied people who had genuine faith, and prayed so hard for the gift of faith. Our minister taught us that if a person does not believe in God, and dies in his unbelief, he cannot go to heaven. Is that true?"

"My son, my Father does not create people with infinite love only to condemn them. He is not a monster. A blind man cannot be punished because he is blind. He searches throughout his whole life trying to find his way. Only if a man has sight and refuses to see can he be blamed for his blindness. Your father, in his blindness, searched his whole life for his way to God, and it was credited to him as faith, just like the people of old before the coming of the Savior. Your father's goodness was his way of saying to God, 'If I knew the way I would follow it.' Do not worry about your father. He is already with my Father in heaven."

THE PARABLE
OF THE CRIMINAL AND THE
RIGHTEOUS POLITICIAN

O F LATE the media have focused on the violence and murder that have become rampant. Cries for strict and swift justice rise up all across the country. State executions are now more popular than ever. Forgiveness and mercy are cries of the radicals and leftists. Looking for approval of this cry for justice, a woman asked Joshua how he felt about executions.

After reminding the crowd of the Gospel story of the woman caught in adultery whom the Pharisees wanted stoned to death, Joshua told the following parable. "A man spent many years of his life fighting for justice. 'I am not a vengeful person,' he would say, 'but there has to be justice if we want to feel safe.' As he was a powerful man with many friends and much money, he influenced legislators to eventually enact laws introducing the death penalty. The governor heartily approved of such a law. Execution was the cry of the day. Jesus' warning 'Let him who is without sin among you cast the first stone' went unheeded. Also his warnings 'Do not judge and you will not be judged,' and 'Unless you forgive, you will not be forgiven,' and 'With what measure you measure out to others, in the same measure will it be measured out to you' were not just empty words spoken by a left-wing God.

"Many years later all those involved, the good and the bad, died. At the judgment they stood before the Judge trembling. Never had they imagined what the Judge was seeing in their hearts. Their whole lives passed before their eyes, as they saw themselves compared to the righteousness of God. Those who had been imprisoned and executed for their crimes came first before the Judge. 'You did great evil in taking the lives of others, for which there is no excuse. You committed other, lesser evils— theft, abuse of others, and robbery. For these you were already severely punished. Though you had repented of your evil ways, you were not allowed to redeem yourselves, as you were judged as evil and condemned to death. As children, you were victims of the cruelty and meanness of others. As you grew older, you were deprived of the means to survive. You were poor and had nothing in your short life. You were despised by the righteous as of no worth. Those who should have shown love and compassion early on brutalized you and blinded your judgment of right and wrong. Though it was no excuse for the evil you have done, divine justice weighs that in the balance. Though you were cruelly treated yourselves, you did many good acts to help others, even while you were in prison. Your sincere repentance before you died has washed away the guilt of your sins, and has won for you God's mercy and compassion. Come into the kingdom prepared for you.'

"Then the Judge called forth the righteous ones. As they stood before him, they expected that they would be praised for their righteousness, especially since the criminals were treated with such mercy. But the Judge looked on them harshly and said to them, 'What am I to do with you, who are so righteous in your own eyes? You saw clearly the evil in others and judged them as evil and of no worth. You despised and condemned and imprisoned the poor. You loved your families, and gave to them generously, but that was self-love, as they were yours. The poor, the hungry, the homeless, and the tortured in spirit, you walked over them in the streets. You called them lazy bums, and worthless wretches, and of no account. They are my children. I put them in your path so you could share with them all the generous gifts I had lavished on you. But you despised them and they died because of your neglect. You voted to execute my children you deemed unfit to live among you. For their deaths you are now called to account. You were in love with money and worshiped daily at the televised tabernacle of rising and falling investments. You kept all the laws, but like the scribes and Pharisees, your hearts were void of love and mercy. You kept my law, but you did not love me. You kept the commandments because they gave you security. Your life was a sham, devoid of substance. Your heart was filled with petty hatreds, and jealousy and mean-spirited spite.

" 'Now you stand before me righteous, and expect praise for your righteous observance of the law. I tell you, there is no room for you here. My home is for those who, in their lives, have shown love and mercy and forgiveness.' "